EXPLORE
MELBOURNE

CONTENTS

BARFLIES

Of all the gin joints in all the towns in all the world… Melbourne has some of the best. Hit Brunswick Street (route 5), St Kilda (route 11) and the city centre laneways (routes 1, route 2 and route 3).

RECOMMENDED ROUTES FOR…

BOHEMIAN MELBOURNE

Call it bohemian, grungy or alternative, this city has art, fashion, music and literary subcultures like no other. To experience them, hang out in Carlton (route 4), Fitzroy (route 5), Flinders Lane (route 3) or St Kilda (route 11).

ETHNIC ENCLAVES

Few cities are as ethnically diverse as Melbourne. Enjoy an espresso in Little Italy (route 4), scoff a bagel with Balaclava's Jewish community (route 11) or try Chinese yum cha in Little Bourke Street (route 2).

FOODIES

This food- and coffee-obsessed city promises a gourmet experience par excellence. The best eateries are in the central city, but there are also gems on Southbank (route 7), in South Yarra (route 9) and St Kilda (route 11).

HISTORY DEVOTEES

See where bushranger Ned Kelly was hanged (route 4), the Royal Australian Navy was established (route 12), the colonial gentry liked to party (route 9) and the world's first narrative film was made (route 2).

MODERN ARCHITECTURE

Melbourne's Victorian-era buildings are marvellous, but the city's modern architecture is even more eye-catching. Don't miss Federation Square or the constructions along Swanston Street (route 3).

THE SEASIDE

If you do love to be beside the seaside, dine overlooking fashionable St Kilda Beach (route 11), bathe at Williamstown Beach (route 12) or set off down the Great Ocean Road (route 14).

SPORTS FANS

Test cricket was born in Melbourne (route 7), which now boasts the year's first tennis Grand Slam (route 7) and Formula One Grand Prix (route 10), while Victoria hosts the world's most famous surfing carnival (route 14).

INTRODUCTION

An introduction to Melbourne's geography, customs and culture, plus illuminating background information on cuisine, history and what to do when you're there.

The Melbourne Safe Deposit building in Queen Street

EXPLORE MELBOURNE

Melbourne is a multi-faceted, multi-cultural, modern metropolis, populated by over four million people who hail from across the globe. Much more laid-back than Sydney, Melbourne has many layers for the inquistive visitor to unwrap.

The city has come a long way since 1835, when farmer John Batman and businessman John Pascoe Fawkner laid down their hats to call it home. It wasn't long before the fledgling settlement became a town and the town became one of the great cities of the southern hemisphere, sped on its way by the discovery of gold and an influx of people from every corner of the globe. Their optimism, ambition and hard work have made Melbourne what it is today.

GEOGRAPHY

Melbourne is the largest city in the state of Victoria, which occupies the southeastern corner of Australia. It is arranged around the shores of Port Phillip Bay, a large inland bay separated from Bass Strait by two elegant arms: the Bellarine Peninsula in the southwest and the Mornington Peninsula in the southeast. Roughly equidistant between the two peninsulas is the mouth of the Yarra River, where Europeans first settled and where the CBD (Central Business District) is located today.

City layout

The inner city covers an area radiating out approximately 7km (4 miles) from the CBD and has an extremely high population density, particularly in the CBD and St Kilda. It is very easy to navigate, with the CBD on the northern banks of the Yarra having been laid out in a grid pattern by surveyor Robert Hoddle in the 1830s.

A number of inner-city suburbs can easily be accessed on foot from the CBD. Just to the north are the parks and tree-lined boulevards of Carlton, as well as the shabby-chic shopping and entertainment strips of neighbouring Fitzroy. Across the Yarra River, beyond the modern developments of Southbank and the green lungs of the Kings Domain and Royal Botanic Gardens, lie the upmarket suburbs of South Melbourne and South Yarra. Other suburbs, such as seaside St Kilda, can be accessed via frequent trams, buses or trains.

Greater Melbourne

The city has one of the largest urban footprints in the world due to its ever-increasing low-density suburban sprawl (it is currently the fastest-grow-

View of the CBD from the banks of the Yarra

ing city in the country, and is tipped to overtake Sydney and become Australia's largest capital city by 2053 if trends continue). Greater Melbourne sprawls eastwards through the wine- and cheese-producing Yarra Valley towards the Dandenong Ranges, and northwards towards the foothills of the Macedon and Great Dividing ranges. It also incorporates the area down to the start of the Mornington Peninsula at Frankston, in the city's southeast, and the satellite suburbs of Werribee and Melton in the west.

ARCHITECTURE

Marvellous Melbourne

Melbourne's foundation and early development corresponded roughly with the rule of Queen Victoria (1819–1901), and much of the inner city's architecture is Victorian in style. Locally, it is sometimes called 'Boom style' architecture, although architectural historians divide it into sub-styles such as Georgian Colonial, Gothic Revival, Renaissance Revival and French Second Empire. The National Trust of Australia (Victoria) has long fought to preserve the unique character of its Victorian streets, declaring many of them Urban Conservation Areas and lobbying the State Government for their preservation and protection. Rows of grand terrace housing adorned with cast-iron lace are scattered throughout the inner city suburbs, often overlooking formal squares and gardens. Terraces

of far more modest workers' cottages – some timber, some brick – also date from this time.

The grand public buildings from this period are quite extraordinary, and make the CBD a veritable treasure trove of 19th-century architecture. Built with gold-rush money, these buildings were often inspired by fashionable buildings in the 'Mother Country', specifically London. Collins Street (see page 28) is full of such buildings. The most significant Victorian-style building in Melbourne is the Royal Exhibition Building in Carlton (see page 50), completed in 1880 and now included on Unesco's World Heritage List.

Art Deco and Modernism

Although there are Edwardian, Art Nouveau and Beaux Arts–style buildings in the city, they are relatively few in number. The next major architectural style to be adopted was Art Deco. Major city thoroughfares including Swanston Street (see page 41) and Bourke Street (see page 34) sport many buildings designed in the Jazz Moderne, Moderne or Streamline Moderne subsets of this style.

The logical design heir to Art Deco was Modernism, and this was another style embraced in Melbourne with alacrity. Orica House (see page 57) is the finest example in central Melbourne, but many buildings at the western end of Collins and Bourke streets are almost as impressive.

Australian icons

Local architects flirted with Brutalism in the 1970s and enjoyed a brief encounter or two with Postmodernism in the 1970s, but it is safe to say that Melbourne's architects and developers have remained faithful to Modernism. In fact, its pared-back, sleek and sophisticated packaging is the very quintessence of the city.

CLIMATE

Melbourne is well known for its changeable weather conditions. This is due in part to the city's flat topography, its situation on Port Phillip Bay and the presence of the Dandenong Ranges to the east, a combination that creates weather systems that often circle the bay.

The city has warm to hot summers. January and February are the hottest months, and the maximum temperature can reach a sweltering 40°C (104°F) and beyond on days when a hot dry wind blows in from the north, straight off the central deserts like a hairdryer in your face. This is bushfire weather, and the scent of smoke often carries on the breeze. The summer's average maximum, however, is a more comfortable 26°C (79°F) and the average minimum is 14°C (57°F). In winter the average maximum temperature is 14°C and the minimum 6°C (43°C), although wind chill can make it seem much cooler. The best time to visit is during autumn or spring, when temperatures are mild and skies relatively clear. However, early or long winters are not unusual.

THE MELBURNIANS

Melbourne is one of the world's most ethnically and culturally diverse cities. Of Greater Melbourne's population of just

A labyrinth of laneways

Every city has a visual signature. Some have a distinctive skyline, others an iconic building or a natural feature. Melbourne has none of these. Instead, the city centre is distinguished by a labyrinth of laneways where graffiti artists work, alternative bars flourish and bohemian boutiques proliferate.

These lanes started life in the 1840s and 1850s as ad hoc service routes to large commercial buildings fronting the major east–west boulevards, and were only traversed by nightsoil carts, delivery vans and rubbish collectors. Today, laneways such as Flinders Lane, Little Collins Street, Little Bourke Street and Little Lonsdale Street are among the most vibrant thoroughfares in the CBD, and the diminutive detours off them are the province of edgy street art and even edgier street cafés and bars.

For a taste of this city phenomenon, check out Oliver Lane, Hosier Lane and Degraves Street between Flinders Lane and Flinders Street; Block Place; and Caledonian Lane between Little Bourke Street and Lonsdale Street.

Colourful public art   *Window cleaning, Fed Square*

over 4 million (the second-largest urban population in Australia after Sydney), almost a third were born overseas. The largest migrant groups come from the UK, Italy, Vietnam, China, New Zealand, Greece, India, South Africa, Sri Lanka and Malaysia, although arrivals from African and Arabic nations such as Sudan, Ethi-opia, Iraq and Iran have been growing in recent years. This heritage is reflected in the rich variety of eating options in the city.

With an average age of 36, Melbourne is a young person's city too, especially in densely populated inner-city areas such as the CBD, South Yarra and St Kilda.

DON'T LEAVE MELBOURNE WITHOUT...

Cramming in some culture. Melbourne is Australia's arty city, and perusing the galleries is a great way to spend a rainy day. Don't miss the National Gallery of Victoria, the Australian Centre for Contemporary Art, Flinders Lane and Gertrude Street. See page 43, page 77, page 44 and page 54.

Experiencing a game of Australian Rules Football. It's a big game, played by big men, but footy is a religion for everyone in Melbourne, young and old, male and female. Go to a game, preferably at the MCG, and see what all the fuss is about. See page 61.

Awakening your inner hipster with a world-class double-shot latte. Melbourne's coffee culture is second to none, and this city's trendy graffiti and cafe-lined laneways are the place to learn the difference between a cappuccino and a macchiato. See page 53.

Exploring the green spaces that punctuate the concrete jungle. Victoria is justly called the 'Garden State', and Melbourne's marvellous gardens include Fitzroy Gardens, Carlton Gardens and the world-re-nowned Royal Botanic. See page 59, page 50 and page 68.

Checking out a live band. 'Keep music live' is a Melbourne mantra and several venues around town have survived the gentrification of the suburbs and the invasion of pokie machines to achieve iconic status, including St Kilda's famously grungy Esplanade Hotel. See page 80.

Learning how to catch a wave. Melbourne's city beaches are fine for sunbathing or swimming, but venture beyond the protective arms of Port Philip Bay to Torquay for world-class surf breaks. See page 93.

Earning a sweat while doing a lap of the Tan. There's isn't a sexier gym anywhere than Melbourne's Botanical Gardens – aka 'the Tan' – where you can join the beautiful people running laps, with eye-candy views over the city and Yarra River. See page 68.

Sipping wine amid the vines. Australia produces some of the planet's best wines, and some fine varietals are made right in the verdant Yarra Valley, where you can do tastings and buy bottles from the cellar door. See page 88.

Runners hit the Tan in the Botanic Gardens

Local culture

Australian culture generally lacks pretensions. You are more likely to be greeted with a 'G'day mate' than a stiff 'How do you do', and while friends and family may kiss cheeks in the European style, mere acquaintances wouldn't dream of doing so, relying instead on firm handshakes to greet both sexes.

Mealtimes generally correspond with those in Britain (lunch between noon–2pm and dinner between 7–9pm). The only difference is that in hot weather, locals tend to eat a bit later and rely heavily on the barbecue. And, with a colourful and eclectic restaurant scene that caters for every palate and purse, locals are just as likely to dine out. Melbourne's coffee culture is world leading, and when ordering a cup in the city's ubiquitous hipster cafés, expect to be bamboozled by a menu of complicated caffeinated options.

Sport is huge in Melbourne, especially footy (Australian Rules, naturally), cricket, swimming, basketball, soccer, netball, golf and athletics. Rugby isn't traditionally big here, but support is slowly growing. Horse racing is a very popular spectator sport, helped by the fact that Melburnians score a public holiday for the Melbourne Cup, known as 'the race that stops a nation', which takes place on the first Tuesday in November at Flemington Racecourse.

But Melbourne is a multi-layered metropolis, and the population doesn't spend all its time chasing balls and bum-ming on beaches. The arts are stronger here than anywhere else in Australia, and the city hosts many cultural festivals, including the Melbourne International Comedy Festival (www.comedyfestival.com.au) each April. In 2008 Melbourne was declared a Unesco City of Literature. An acknowledgement of the city's strong literary culture and heritage, the accolade has led to the establishment of the Wheeler Centre (www.wheelercentre.com) at the State Library (see page 45), dedicated to the discussion and promotion of writing, books and ideas. The popular Melbourne Writers' Festival (www.mwf.com.au) is held in August each year.

A LIVEABLE CITY

The Mercer Quality of Living Survey and *The Economist* World's Most Liveable Cities Index regularly rate Melbourne highly. It's easy to see why. The city's air is clean, its suburbs are green and its streets are safe. Public transport is good and, while the cost of living is high, so are wages. Melbourne's diverse population endows day-to-day life with a cultural richness, inclusivity and complexity seen in very few Western societies; it has thriving arts and sports scenes; and its focus on the enjoyable elements of life – including outdoor activities and some of the world's best food, wine and coffee – make it a truly fabulous place in which to work, live or stay.

Variety Entertainers of the Century Mosaic at Docklands

TOP TIPS FOR VISITING MELBOURNE

Take the tram. Australia isn't a cheap place to travel, but a fantastic exception in Melbourne comes in the shape of the No. 35 City Circle tram, a free service run for visitors. The tram departs Flinders Street every 12 minutes 10am–6pm Sun–Wed and 10am–9pm Thur–Sat, and does a loop around the city taking in many major tourist sights.

Local hotties. Backyard barbecues are a way of life for suburban Melburnians, but you don't need a backyard to cook up an alfresco storm – there are free barbecues in public parks all over the city, including Birrarung Marr, on the city's riverbank.

On your bike. To see more of Melbourne's streetscape, take advantage of the city's Bike Share scheme. For a subscription of $2.90 per day you can pick up a bike (and a courtesy helmet, because head protection is compulsory) from a host of bike stations around the city and use it for a short period. See www.melbournebike-share.com.au for more.

Four seasons. Famously, Melbourne will throw all manner of weather at you in the space of a few hours, let alone a whole day, so be prepared. When heading out for the day, dress in layers, always have something warm and waterproof, and pack an umbrella.

Home James. Since 2008 it has been compulsory to pay taxi fares upfront between the hours of 10pm and 5am. The advantage of this is that you know exactly what your ride is going to cost. You can access a standard fare calculator online.

Bus to the sky. Tullamarine International Airport has no rail link. A taxi from the CBD will cost you somewhere north of $50, but Skybus (www.skybus.com.au) run a 24-hour service between Southern Cross Station and the airport that costs adults $18 single, or $30 return.

Wait for the green man. In Melbourne it's illegal to jaywalk, ie to cross the road when you're not at a pedestrian crossing. This law is broken thousands of times a day, but occasionally police will pull people up for it, and you can be fined.

Welcome to the cheap seats. 'Tightarse Tuesday' is a concept whereby tickets to all kinds of shows and events are discounted on Tuesday evenings. Look out for Tuesday bargains on everything from cinema tickets to entry to top acts during the excellent Melbourne International Comedy Festival.

Tourism angels. If someone dressed in red approaches you while you're looking lost and confused on a street corner in the CBD and asks if you need help, don't worry. These are City Ambassadors – volunteers who will help you find your way around town. They are typically found along Swanston Street, at corners such as Flinders Street and Bourke Street, between 10am and 4pm.

Summer break. Many businesses close down from Christmas Day until mid-January, during which time Melburnians decamp along the coast for their annual – and sacrosanct – beach holiday.

Head to David's for Chinese food

FOOD AND DRINK

In recent years, Australia has become as renowned as an destination for its cuisine as for its natural attractions. Each of the capital cities has a great food scene, but Melbourne's has long been considered the king of them all.

Restaurants in Melbourne function as global culinary incubators; many young chefs train locally and then leave for further experience on foreign shores. The favour is returned by scores of overseas chefs who do the opposite and make their lives and careers here after training with top-notch restaurants around the world. These talented imports are lured here by peerless fresh produce, exciting fusions of flavours, a devoted foodie culture and an attitude to fine dining that stresses fun rather than formality.

MELBOURNE'S CUISINE

There's no one tag for Melbourne's cuisine. Here you can eat everything from classic French dishes to spicy Malaysian hawker food, simple Mediterranean favourites to molecular tours de force à la Heston Blumenthal. The only thing that's uniform is the excellence of the local food and wine – indulging your tastebuds here is a supremely satisfying experience – and, although it doesn't always come cheap, the variety of the selection means there is something sensational to suit most budgets.

Fresh produce

Fresh, locally sourced produce is used by chefs across the city, with many having a particular penchant for organic artisan ingredients. Menus are likely to specify meat producers (grass-fed and Wagyu beef from East Gippsland is favoured), the provenance of cheese (look out for offerings from Gippsland and the Yarra Valley), where salt is sourced (the pink grains from Murray River are often used) and the waters from which seafood has been sourced (Pacific oysters and Coffin Bay scallops from neighbouring South Australia are hugely popular).

For cooks, the quality and availability of fresh local ingredients is superb. Melbourne is known throughout Australia for the excellence of its fresh produce markets. The best of these is the historic Queen Victoria Market, South Melbourne Market and Prahran Market, all of which are home to hundreds of specialist food stalls. There are also many farmers' markets around town, including the Slow Food Melbourne Farmers' Market (www.mfm.com.au) at the Abbotsford Convent on the fourth Saturday of every month.

Sweet treats   *Deli produce at Queen Victoria Market*

International cuisine

The Italian, French and Chinese (specifically Cantonese) cuisines have long pedigrees in Melbourne, but food from Spain, Lebanon, Morocco, Thailand, Malaysia, Turkey, Vietnam and Ethiopia is becoming increasingly popular, and many of the city's most exciting restaurants showcase these cuisines.

Brilliantly, Australian chefs will often draw on cuisines from across the globe for inspiration when putting together a menu. A fragrant red Thai curry might sit next to a perfectly char-grilled rib-eye served with mash, and a delicate panna cotta might share the spotlight with mango-topped sticky rice.

WHERE TO EAT

Some cuisines are strongly associated with particular streets or suburbs – Footscray and Richmond are full of Vietnamese restaurants, for instance – but this is less the case now than it has been in the past. Most suburbs have eating options in every budget category, although restaurants at the higher end of the spectrum tend to be found in central Melbourne, South Yarra and St Kilda.

The local foodie bible is the Good Food Guide (www.goodfood.com.au) published by *The Age*. Each year the guide's food critics award chef hats (a star equivalent) to the best eateries in Victoria. The ultimate accolade is a three-hat rating, but a one- or two-hat rating is also impressive, ensuring both clients and the respect of the food-and-wine community.

High-end restaurants

Australians are an egalitarian bunch and tend to view formal fine-dining establishments with a certain degree of suspicion. Epicures are just as likely to get excited about the menu at an edgy inner-suburban tapas bar as they are at restaurants in possession of a rare three-hat rating, and those who dine out regularly tend to focus their attention on one- or two-hat establishments.

Only three restaurants in town boast three-hat status: Attica in Ripponlea, Flower Drum in China Town, and Vue de Monde in central Melbourne. All offer simply extraordinary dining experiences. These places are expensive – set menus hover around A$150 per person – and have wonderful wine lists. You will need to book ahead.

There is a slew of upscale restaurants at Crown Casino too, including Nobu, Spice Temple, Rockpool Bar & Grill and Bistro Guillaume. St Kilda has Circa at The Prince hotel, South Yarra has The Botanical and central Melbourne has Taxi Dining Room in Federation Square and ezard at The Adelphi hotel. You should dress to impress at all of these, and also come with a fully charged credit card.

Mediterranean–style lunch

Mid-range restaurants

This is the category that Melburnians love the most. Often, the food on offer is just as impressive as that served in the high-end establishments, the differences being that the vibe will be more casual, the wine lists less encyclopaedic, the service less formal and the prices more reasonable. The vast majority offer menus heavy on Mediterranean choices, with occasional forays into Asia.

Many of these places match a stylish interior with an impressive menu, interesting wine list and professional service. Two-hat places sitting comfortably in this category include Grossi Florentino, Café Di Stasio and Matteo's.

Ethnic restaurants

In times past, describing a Melbourne restaurant as 'ethnic' hinted at over-spiced dishes (usually with Indian overtones), a hippie interior and Ravi Shankar on the sound system. Not any more, though. Supreme among the quality restaurants offering specific ethnic cuisine are the Spanish MoVida, pan-Asian Gingerboy, Thai Longrain and Lebanese/Persian Rumi. Meanwhile, *yum cha* (dim sum) is a weekend institution, as is a pre-dinner tapas indulgence or an antipasti-fuelled *aperitivo* in an inner-city bar/restaurant.

Excellent takeaway food is also on offer here. Streets such as Sydney Road in Brunswick are littered with places specialising in cheap and tasty falafel sandwiches and *pides*, and you will find rice-paper rolls and *pho* (noodle soup) in many Footscray and Richmond cafés. Good sushi can generally be sourced all over town.

Pubs

The phenomenon of the gastro pub hasn't really hit Melbourne. Instead, many corner pubs across the inner city have been reinvented as attitude-free drinking zones that have undergone funky fitouts and offer well-priced and imaginative bar meals. Notable examples include The Lincoln Hotel in Carlton, the Middle Park Hotel opposite Albert Park, the Railway in South Melbourne and The Builder's Arms in Fitzroy, but there are many others where the menu is more likely to feature a spicy calamari stir-fry or fragrant chicken tagine and couscous as it is a plate of steak, eggs and chips. Those pubs with a beer garden tend to be hugely popular in summer.

DRINKS

Beer

Most Aussies like a beer, but international visitors had best brace themselves when they first go to the bar, as Australia has become one of the most expensive places to go out drinking in the world. A pint of beer will almost always put at least a $10 hole in your wallet. Prices in bottleshops are more reasonable.

At one time the choice was pretty limited – you either drank Victoria

Aussie lager

Bitter (VB) or Carlton Draught, or you went thirsty – but these days the craft ale and boutique beer tide has well and truly washed across Melbourne's inner city pubs and reached the bars of the trendier suburbs. Mountain Goat, Thunder Road and Broo are three popular Victoria-based brewing companies, and you will often find their beers available on tap, or at least in bottles. Other tasty interstate alternatives include Cooper's (South Australia), Boags and Cascade (both Tasmania), and Little Creatures (Western Australia). Imported beers are also widely available.

Beer is served in three glass sizes: a glass (200ml), pot (285ml) or pint (typically 500ml).

Wine

Australia is one of the most highly respected New World wine-producing countries. Regions such as the Barossa, Coonawarra, Clare Valley, Margaret River, Yarra Valley and Mornington Peninsula produce exceptionally fine varietals year after year, and these are enthusiastically stocked by local restaurants. Despite Australian's beer-swilling reputation, many Melburnians are well clued up about their wines, and are just as likely to order a glass of shiraz or sauvignon blanc when they go out for a drink as they are an ale or cocktail. Those keen to sample Victorian wines should opt for shiraz from the Heathcote region, pinot noir, chardonnay or spar-

kling wine from the Yarra Valley, or pinot noir or chardonnay from the Mornington Peninsula, Bellarine Peninsula and Gippsland. Purchased in bottleshops, Australian wine can be extremely reasonably priced, and some restaurants allow you to BYO (bring your own) – although they may charge you a corkage fee.

Coffee

Melbourne has one of the most established coffee cultures in the world, and baristas trained here have gone on to create caffeine-laced waves of enthusiasm for Australian-style coffee across much bigger cities, such as London. The way the beans are roasted and ground has become a fine art, and then there's myriad ways to serve the final product. Trendy cafés in suburbs such as Fitzroy and South Melbourne lead the way here, and visitors may find themselves happy converts to the coffee cult that thrives in these laneways.

Food and drink prices

Throughout this guide, we have used the following price ranges to denote the approximate costs of a two-course dinner for one with a glass of house wine:

$$$$ = over A$80
$$$ = A$60–80
$$ = A$45–60
$ = below A$45

Boomerangs hand-crafted by Aboriginal Australians

SHOPPING

Melbourne is known as Australia's fashion capital and shopping mecca, and style-conscious citizens of other Australian cities have always flocked here in search of something special from the 'burbs boutiques, or a bargain in the factory outlets.

The local shopping scene is distinctive, with plenty of quirky boutiques, designer outlets and gourmet food stores, while malls and chain stores tend to be on the city's outer fringe. Locals have turned shopping into an art form – they know where to find the most attractive designer jewellery, the hippest homewares and the edgiest ensembles. Sartorial gurus are particularly in evidence during the Melbourne Fashion Festival (www.lmff.com.au) each March.

SHOPPING AREAS

Central Melbourne
Central Melbourne is home to the Myer and David Jones department stores, the fashionable GPO and QV shopping centres, global luxury brands such as Chanel and Gucci, and lots of boutique book retailers.

Small designer boutiques cluster in the city's laneways, streets and arcades. For Australian-designed jewellery, e.g.etal in Flinders Lane is hard to beat, while for a wide-brimmed Akubra hat, City Hatters at Flinders Street Station is the place to go. Fashionable accessories from Australia and overseas tempt anyone who ventures into Christine, and stylish hand-made jewellery items, textiles, glass, ceramic and timber works by designers crowd the shelves at Craft, formerly Craft Victoria – both are located on Flinders Lane. It's not all good news for window shoppers and fans of brick-and-mortar retail, however, with several edgy names in Melbourne's fashion world – including Genki and Alice Euphemia – having shut their doors in recent years, to trade exclusively online.

Gertrude and Brunswick Streets
Accessories, toiletries and alternative and vintage fashion are strongly represented in Fitzroy. Australia's famous Crumpler brand has its flagship bag store on Gertrude Street, and its neighbours include local brand Aesop, known for its natural skin, hair and body products. Further west is the unassuming Cottage Industry, a fashion and accessory store that balances charm, style and affordability with great success.

Brunswick Street has boutiques galore, including the exquisite Kleins Perfumery and quirky Koko jewellery store. Other favourites include Douglas and Hope for fashion and homewares,

Boutique shops and cafés line a laneway

and T2 for tea and tea-making accessories. Simon Johnson, in nearby St David Street, is the place to go for Australian and imported gourmet foods.

Chapel Street
Come to Chapel Street in Prahran for local fashion labels Alannah Hill and Scanlan & Theodore. Travel southwards to find the funky Chapel Street Bazaar, home to vintage furniture and bric-a-brac. Foodies flock to The Essential Ingredient, in Prahran Market on Commercial Road, which stocks a huge range of gourmet foods and homewares.

High Street and Malvern Road
This is where you will find antiques and designer homewares. These chichi strips – running parallel through Prahran, Armadale and Malvern – are where ladies lunch. Big names include Graham Geddes Antiques and John D. Dunn Antiques in Malvern Road. Fashion boutiques worth checking out include Husk in Malvern Road.

This is also where the art and antiques auction houses are located. Bonhams & Goodman is on Malvern Road in Prahran, Leonard Joel is on Malvern Road in South Yarra, Philips Auctions is on Glenferrie Road in Malvern and Sotheby's is on High Street in Armadale.

Coventry Street
Homewares are strongly represented on the stretch of Coventry Street between Clarendon and Cecil streets in South Melbourne. Look out for Nest (on Coventry Street), Macphees for the Wine Enthusiast (on Buckhurst Street) and Made in Japan (on Coventry Street).

Bookshop bonanza

Melbourne is well known for its impressive independent bookshops. Chief among these are the five stores in the Readings group, located in Carlton, St Kilda, Hawthorn, Malvern and the State Library of Victoria. The flagship Carlton store is one of the city's main literary salons, hosting book launches and literary events galore.

Other stores well worth a browse include Reader's Feast on the corner of Swanston and Bourke streets in the CBD, The Avenue Bookstore in Albert Park, The Paperback Bookshop and Hill of Content stores at the top end of Bourke Street in the CBD, and the Brunswick Street Bookstore in Fitzroy. Collectors of antiquarian books gravitate towards Kay Craddock in Collins Street, gay and lesbian readers adore Hares & Hyenas in Fitzroy and poetry lovers linger among the shelves at Collected Works in Swanston Street's Nicholas Building. A good chain bookshop is Dymocks at 234 Collins Street, while the Foreign Language Bookstore at 259 Collins Street stocks books in over 100 different languages.

The Fed Square Book Market serves a weekly feast of 5,000 new and pre-loved titles to bibliophiles every Saturday between 11am and 5pm.

Live music at the Ding Dong Lounge

ENTERTAINMENT

Often described as Australia's cultural capital, Melbourne takes live music, art and entertainment seriously. It's rare to encounter a night when a cutting-edge performance of one type or another isn't being staged around town.

The opening-night scene dominates the city's highbrow social calendar, and a decent allocation of local-, state- and federal-government money is dedicated to the performing arts. Many directors have done their artistic apprenticeships here and gone on to work overseas, recent examples being Jonathan Mills (Director of the Edinburgh International Festival) and Barrie Kosky (Chief Director at the Komische Oper in Berlin). Hundreds of local performers do stay in Melbourne, attracted by the diversity of work, appreciative audiences and excellent venues.

The best listings for Melbourne's lively performing arts scene can be found in the Entertainment Guide (EG) published every Friday in *The Age* (www.theage.com.au/entertainment). For discounted tickets to various live performances, visit the Halftix (www.halftixmelbourne.com) box office by the Town Hall on Swanston Street. Tickets are usually sold on the day of the performance and only cash payments are accepted.

ARTS FESTIVALS

Melbourne's flagship cultural event, the Melbourne International Arts Festi-

val (www.melbournefestival.com.au), is held in October and features a world-class line-up of theatre, music, dance and visual arts. Other festivals include the Melbourne International Comedy Festival (www.comedyfestival.com.au) March–April, the Melbourne International Jazz Festival (www.melbournejazz.com) usually May–June, and the Melbourne Fringe Festival (www.melbournefringe.com.au) September–October.

THEATRE

Melbourne has a vibrant theatre scene. The major professional company is the Melbourne Theatre Company (www.mtc.com.au), its productions appearing in two venues – the MTC Theatre at Southbank and the Arts Centre at St Kilda Road. The state's second company is the Malthouse Theatre (www.malthousetheatre.com.au) on Sturt Street in Southbank.

Theatrical events including musicals are staged at the Arts Centre (www.artscentremelbourne.com.au), Her Majesty's Theatre (www.hmt.com.au) and the Princess, Regent and Comedy theatres (www.marrinertheatres.com.au) in the city cen-

The Malthouse theatre   *Posters in Las Chicas café in St Kilda*

tre. Adventurous work can be found at fortyfivedownstairs (www.fortyfivedownstairs.com) in Flinders Lane, Red Stitch Actors' Theatre (www.redstitch.net) in East St Kilda, La Mama (www.lamama.com.au) in Carlton and Theatreworks (www.theatreworks.org.au) in St Kilda.

DANCE

The Melbourne-based national ballet company, the Australian Ballet (www.australianballet.com.au) performs at the Arts Centre's State Theatre. Chunky Move (www.chunkymove.com) is known internationally for its programme of genre-defying dance performance. It usually performs at the Malthouse Theatre.

MUSIC

Rock and indie
Melbourne's live music scene is largely based in pub venues. To check who's playing in town, check EG and tune into local radio stations 3RRR (102.7 FM), 3PBS (106.7 FM) and 3MMM (105.1 FM), and national station triple j (www.abc.net.au/triplej), whose website has excellent listings. Big-name acts play at venues such as the Palais in St Kilda (www.palaistheatre.net.au), Festival Hall (www.festivalhall.com.au) in the city, and Melbourne's many enormous sporting areas, but The Esplanade Hotel (The Espy; www.espy.com.au) and Prince Bandroom (www.princebandroom.com.au) in St Kilda host local, interstate and international acts.

Classical and jazz
The Melbourne Symphony Orchestra (www.mso.com.au) is Australia's oldest orchestra and has an excellent reputation. It performs at a variety of locations, including the Melbourne Town Hall and the Arts Centre. In summer it performs free concerts at the Sidney Myer Music Bowl. Other classical concerts are staged at the Melbourne Recital Centre (www.melbournerecital.com.au) on Southbank Boulevard.

The Australian Art Orchestra (www.aao.com.au) is the country's premier contemporary music ensemble. Although based in Sydney, Opera Australia (www.opera-australia.org.au) has Melbourne seasons at the Arts Centre's State Theatre in April–June and October–December.

For jazz, the main venues in town are Bennetts Lane (www.bennettslane.com) and Dizzy's (www.dizzys.com.au) in Richmond.

FILM

Melbourne has a strong arthouse cinema scene, with popular venues including Cinema Nova (www.cinemanova.com.au) in Carlton, Kino Cinemas (www.palacecinemas.com.au) in the city centre, and the Como in South Yarra (www.palacecinemas.com.au).

The high-profile Melbourne International Film Festival (www.melbournefilmfestival.com.au) is held in July and August each year at venues across central Melbourne.

Aussie Rules footy

SPORTING EVENTS

Melburnians may enjoy cultural pursuits, but they enjoy sport even more. Woe betide those who publicly profess to have no interest in tennis, cricket and football – their stance will be met by a mixture of disbelief and disdain by the ball-mad majority.

There's something endearing about the general obsession with spectator sport here, and locals have truly got it down to an art form. They know that the Melbourne Cricket Ground's Southern Stand is where they should be on Boxing Day, that they should take a foldout chair when queuing for tickets to the Australian Football League's finals series and that sunblock and bottled water are essential when spectating in summer. If attending a major sporting event while in town, you are bound to be bowled over by the infectious enthusiasm, fierce partisanship and general bonhomie evident in the crowd – and the fact that the terraces are typically shared by fans of opposing teams with very little trouble ever erupting.

AUSTRALIAN RULES FOOTBALL

The AFL (Australian Football League) season starts in March each year and culminates in the finals series in September. Melbourne goes footy crazy during the finals – club colours are seen everywhere, pubs show televised matches on big screens, finals barbe-

cues are popular and there's a street parade in central Melbourne on the Friday before the Grand Final. The Grand Final itself is played at the MCG on the last Saturday of the month before a crowd of 100,000. Unfortunately, tickets for all finals matches are extremely hard to come by; for more information see www.afl.com.au/tickets.

AUSTRALIAN F1 GRAND PRIX

Locals are divided when it comes to this event – fans are loud in their support and opponents are even louder in voicing their displeasure (although everyone is drowned out by the cacophony of the race itself). Held in the typically tranquil surrounds of Albert Park Lake in March, the four-day event (www.grandprix.com.au) certainly causes a buzz around town, particularly on Lygon Street in Carlton, home to a huge concentration of Ferrari fans.

SPRING RACING CARNIVAL

On the first Tuesday in November, thousands of Melburnians don their smartest clobber (including a hat), grab a form guide and head to Flemington Race-

Melburnians are sport mad

course and one of the world's great horse races, the Melbourne Cup (www.melbournecup.com). Those who don't attend in person gather around TVs in pubs and at barbecues all around the city and suburbs (and country).

Other popular Spring Carnival events are Oaks Day and Derby Day at Flemington (www.vrc.net.au), the Caulfield Cup at Caulfield Racecourse (www.melbourneracingclub.net.au) and the Cox Plate at Moonee Valley Racecourse (www.mvrc.net.au).

TENNIS

The Australian Open (www.australianopen.com) is perennially popular. The Grand Slam tournament for the Asia/Pacific region is held in the second half of January each year at Melbourne Park on the Yarra. The world's best slog it out in often sweltering conditions (40°C/104°F is not unusual) and the crowd is vociferous in its support of local contenders and visiting favourites.

TEST CRICKET

Summer in Melbourne means two things: beach and cricket (often combined in the popular pastime of beach cricket). The Boxing Day Test at the MCG is the most famous date on the international cricket calendar, and when the traditional foe, England, come to town to fight for the Ashes, the atmosphere is immense. For more, visit www.cricket.com.au.

FOOTBALL (SOCCER)

The Australian A-League (www.a-league.com.au) was established in in 2004 and, although clubs still struggle to retain their brightest talent when European sides come calling, it has raised the profile and quality of the world game here. The season runs October–May, and Melbourne has two sides in the 10-team league, Melbourne Victory and Melbourne City – both based at AAMI. Derby games have the best atmosphere.

GOLF

Melbourne boasts some world-class greens, including Royal Melbourne (www.royalmelbourne.com.au), a 36-hole club in Black Rock, which is Australia's premier course and has twice hosted the Presidents Cup. Fancy playing a round with kangaroos for an audience? Try Anglesea Golf Course.

BEACH EVENTS

Summer sees a riot of kayak, SUP and surfski paddling races, ocean swims, Surf Life Saving events and action-packed beach festivals. Victoria's famous Great Ocean Road hosts two high-profile sporting events each year – The Rip Curl Pro Surf (www.ripcurl.com.au) at Easter and the Lorne Pier to Pub swim (www.lornesurfclub.com.au/Content/PierToPub) in January.

HISTORY: KEY DATES

In 1835 John Batman stood on the banks of the Yarra and noted, 'This will be the place for a village.' Two decades later, a gold rush caused the settlement to boom and become the 'Marvellous Melbourne' that it has been ever since.

EUROPEAN ARRIVALS

1802	The crew of the Lady Nelson are the first white men to enter the Port Phillip Bay area.
1834	Pastoralists (livestock farmers) from Van Diemen's Land establish Victoria's first long-term settlement at Portland on Bass Strait.
1835	Farmer John Batman makes a treaty with the Wurundjeri for 240,000 hectares (592,800 acres) of land on Port Phillip's shores, giving them blankets and trinkets in payment; Batman and businessman John Pascoe Fawkner then founds a white settlement on the banks of the Yarra River.
1837	The settlement is named in honour of British Prime Minister Lord Melbourne; surveyor Robert Hoddle lays out central Melbourne's grid system; the first inner-city land sale.
1842	The municipality of Melbourne is created.
1845	The Princes Bridge is constructed, linking the north and south banks of the Yarra River.
1847	Queen Victoria declares Melbourne a city.

GOLD RUSH

1851	Melbourne is separated from New South Wales; gold is discovered in central Victoria, triggering a gold rush.
1852	75,000 gold-seekers arrive in the colony.
1854	A railway between Port Melbourne and the central city is opened.
1858	The first games of Aussie Rules Football are played.
1861	The Melbourne Cup is held for the first time – won by the horse Archer.
1877	The first Test cricket match is played at the MCG.

Melbourne as a young settlement in 1838, prior to the gold rush

1880	Notorious bushranger Ned Kelly is captured in Glenrowan and hanged in Melbourne; the International Exhibition is held in the newly built Royal Exhibition Building.
1885	The first cable-tram line opens.

20TH CENTURY

1901	The federation of the six colonies becomes the Commonwealth of Australia; Melbourne is made temporary parliamentary capital.
1906	The Melbourne Symphony Orchestra is formed.
1927	Federal parliament moves to the new national capital, Canberra.
1933	Melbourne's population passes 1 million mark.
1942	Melbourne becomes the Allied headquarters for the Southwest Pacific in World War II.
1945	Australia embarks on an immigration programme; Melbourne attracts migrants from Greece, Italy and Malta.
1956	The Olympic Games are held in Melbourne.
1961	Melbourne's population passes 2 million.
1973	The 'White Australia' policy is overturned and Melbourne sees a huge increase in immigrants from Southeast Asia.
1990	Southbank Promenade is completed, opening the city to the southern banks of the Yarra.
1996	Development of the Docklands begins.

21ST CENTURY

2002	Federation Square opens.
2006	Melbourne hosts Commonwealth Games.
2008	Prime Minister Kevin Rudd officially apologises to Aboriginal Australians of the 'Stolen Generations'.
2009	Bushfires sweep through many parts of Victoria, including the Yarra Valley; deaths total nearly 200.
2010	Julia Gillard, a Welsh-born Australian, becomes the first female prime minister of Australia.
2013	Tony Abbott, leader of the Liberal Party, becomes prime minister.
2014	A bridge named after Jim Stynes, an Irish AFL legend, is opened across the Yarra; Labor win a landslide victory in Victoria.

BEST ROUTES

Atrium at 161 On Collins

COLLINS STREET

Aficionados of architecture will be in seventh heaven as they stroll the length of this famous city street. An open museum of significant 19th- and 20th-century buildings, including opulent Block Arcade and the Rialto Towers, it is also known for the plane trees, upmarket shops and cafés that punctuate the Paris End.

> **DISTANCE:** 2km (1.25 miles)
> **TIME:** Six hours
> **START:** Southern Cross Railway Station
> **END:** City Museum
> **POINTS TO NOTE:** Combine this with routes 2 and 3 for a rewarding two-day exploration of central Melbourne.

Named after Lieutenant-Governor David Collins, who led the unsuccessful attempt to settle at Sorrento (on the Mornington Peninsula, south of Melbourne) in 1803, Collins Street has always been the business end of the city. Melbourne's stock exchange has been located here since its foundation in 1884, and banks and insurance agents started trading from Collins Street premises as early as 1838. Today, Collins Street is recognised as the grande dame of Melbourne's boulevards, and the majority of its buildings are protected by heritage legislation.

SOUTHERN CROSS STATION

Begin in front of **Southern Cross Railway Station ❶**, designed by British architect Nicholas Grimshaw in association with local firm Daryl Jackson. Completed in 2006, it has won a swag of national and international architectural awards. With

Rialto Towers   *Mosaic evoking Collins Street's history*

its massive scale, airy interior and sensuously undulating roof, the building has endowed the western gateway to the city centre with the visual gravitas it has long deserved. The coach terminal to the rear of Grimshaw's structure is a less-inspired addition from a visual perspective, but the retail side of the complex continues to evolve, with Bourke Street Bridge the newest section to host shops and restaurants. From the station, walk east into Collins Street.

SPENCER STREET TO WILLIAM STREET

Lovers of Modernist architecture from the early 20th century will appreciate the **Former McPherson's Hardware Showrooms** ❷ at 546–566 Collins Street. The curves of this 1935–6 building may be subtler than those of Southern Cross Station, but they pack quite a visual punch, especially when married with the elongated horizontal form of the building's glossy black tiles and profusion of glass.

Rialto Precinct

From the King Street corner, you will see the towering glass **Rialto Towers** ❸ on your right. Completed in 1986, the towers were for many years the tallest structure in Australia, famous for their sunset-reflecting mirrored glass. Now trumped in height by Eureka Tower, they're still arguably the city's best-recognised landmarks. The renowned three-hat restaurant **Vue de Monde** (see page 112) has taken over the former observation deck on the 55th floor of the Rialto Towers after relocating from Little Collins Street.

Cowering at the towers' base, at 497–503 Collins Street, are the charming 1891 **Rialto** and **Winfield buildings**, once home to offices, warehouse space and the Melbourne Wool Exchange, but now occupied by the refurbished Intercontinental Melbourne Hotel (previously the Rialto Hotel). At the Towers' forecourt, adjacent to the hotel is **Merchant** (see page 111), another restaurant by famous chef Guy Grossi. East of the Winfield Building are the façades of the **New Zealand Insurance Build-**

The Immigration Museum

ing (483–485 Collins Street), **Record Chambers** (479–481 Collins Street) and Olderfleet (471–477 Collins Street). The Venetian Gothic-style Insurance Building dates from 1888 and is sited next to the French Renaissance–style Record Chambers, which predates it by one year. Best of all, though, is the over-the-top Gothic Revival façade of the Olderfleet, designed by William Pitt (who also designed the Rialto Building) in 1889. Sadly, most of the fabric of these buildings was lost in 1985, replaced by a glass office block.

WILLIAM STREET TO QUEEN STREET

Past William Street you enter the city's banking and financial precinct, presided over by muscular office towers, such as the **Royal Insurance Building** ❹ (430–444 Collins Street). Dating from 1965, this is the first in a series of exceptionally fine Modernist office buildings designed by local architectural firm Yuncken Freeman. Also of note in this block is the imposing Renaissance Revival bulk of the former **Bank of Australasia** building on the northwestern corner of Queen Street and Goode House (the old **National Mutual Building**) on the southwestern corner. The latter, a Gothic Revival office block completed in 1893, is often described as one of the city's first skyscrapers.

If you're in need of a feed, veer left into Bank Place and find **Syracuse**, see

❶, or carry on and turn right into Little Collins Street to reach **Café Vue**, see ❷.

Immigration Museum detour

Back on Collins Street, if you detour south into Market Street and walk two blocks downhill, you'll reach one of Melbourne's major 19th-century public buildings, the **Customs House** ❺. This classically proportioned building was constructed in two stages between 1856 and 1876 on a site near the city's port. It now houses the **Immigration Museum** (400 Flinders Street; www.museumvictoria.com.au/immigration-museum; daily 10am–5pm; charge for adults, children free), which hosts a rotating exhibition programme exploring the often sobering, but always fascinating, stories of the many migrants who have settled in Victoria.

QUEEN STREET TO ELIZABETH STREET

The jewel in the crown of the banking district, which extends into this next block, is the **ANZ Gothic Bank** ❻ (Mon–Fri 9.30am–4pm) on the northeastern corner of Queen Street. Built 1883–7, its exterior sports Gothic porches and delicate stone carvings, while the exquisite banking chamber known as the Cathedral Room features beautiful iron columns and sculptural capitals. There are information points inside the building that facilitate self-guided tours through the Cathedral

Displays in the museum   *Buildings on Bank Place*

Room and **ANZ Banking Museum** (Mon–Fri 10am–3pm; free).

Near the northwestern corner of Elizabeth Street is the city's most famous gentlemen's outfitter, **Henry Bucks** (www.henrybucks.com.au), which has traded in the city for 125 years.

THE BLOCK

Situated between Elizabeth and Swanston streets, 'The Block' is almost as prestigious an address today as it was in its late 19th-century heyday. Then, colonial banks lined the southern side of Collins Street, and fashionable shops could be found on the northern side. In the late 19th century and early 20th century, Melburnians donned their finest outfits to 'Do the Block' on Saturday afternoons. The pivot of their promenade was the opulent **Block Arcade 7** (282 Collins Street; www.theblockarcade.com.au), built 1891–3. The ornate Victorian façade of this building is impressive, but the wow factor kicks in upon viewing the opulent interior, with its ornate shopfronts, glass skylights, mosaic-tiled floor and octangular core. Inside is a Melbourne institution, the **Hopetoun Tearooms**, see **3**, which has been serving its famous pinwheel sandwiches and 'lamingtons' (spongecake squares covered with chocolate and coconut and sometimes filled with cream) for over a century. Behind the arcade, accessed through its northern rear entrance, is **Block Place**, a narrow laneway full of hip cafés and boutiques.

On the southern side of Collins Street, on the corner of Manchester Lane, look out for the gorgeous gilt-and-glass mosaic on the façade of **Newspaper House 8** (247–249 Collins Street), once the headquarters of Melbourne's major evening newspaper. Created by Napier Waller, the three panels depict modern advances in communication and transport. The text – 'I'll put a girdle around about the earth' – is amazingly prescient, considering it dates from 1932, long before global media empires achieved exactly that.

SWANSTON STREET TO RUSSELL STREET

The stretch from Swanston Street to Russell Street follows a relatively steep incline, and is notable for its concentration of churches and theatres.

Next door to the **Melbourne Town Hall** is the **Melbourne Athenaeum 9**. In the 19th century, many municipalities in Victoria established Mechanics Institutes aimed at providing blue-collar workers ('mechanics') with self-improvement tools such as libraries. An institute at 184–192 Collins Street was the first of these to open (in 1839) and its original modest building was replaced by this Renaissance Revival structure in 1886. The **subscription library** (www.melbourneathenaeum.org.au; Mon–Tue, Thur–Fri 9.30am–5pm, Wed 11am–7pm, Sat 9.30am–1pm) on the mezzanine level still operates.

Haighs Chocolate Store in Block Arcade

Across the road from the Athenaeum is the **Regent Theatre** (www.marriner theatres.com.au), a grand picture palace built in 1928 that now stages live shows.

THE PARIS END

The stretch between Russell and Spring streets became known as the 'Paris End' of Collins Street after the Oriental Hotel at No. 17 (since demolished) opened Melbourne's first sidewalk café in the 1950s. These were the days when glamorous society ladies flocked to **Le Louvre**, the über glamorous boutique that occupied a small 19th century townhouse at 74 Collins Street, until it recently moved to trendy South Yarra. While they were being fitted, their spouses sealed business deals over cigars at the **Melbourne Club** ⑩, (36 Collins Street), an old-school gentlemen's club established in 1838, and housed since 1858 in this building, which has been graced by many notables, including Robert O'Hara Burke, the explorer who allegedly left on his ill-fated expedition without paying his debts, but ended up with his portrait on the wall after a heroic demise.

Georgian Revival townhouses
There are many gracious Georgian Revival buildings along this strip, many of which started life as private residences for medical practitioners, bankers, solicitors and dentists. Then, as now, a Collins Street address sig-

nified professional respectability and success.

The buildings at the top end of the street are particularly handsome – look out for **Portland House**, a townhouse and doctor's surgery dating from 1872, and **Alcaston House**, the only early multi-storey apartment building remaining in the central city. It dates from 1929–30 and is still a blue-chip residential address.

On the southern side of the street, at No. 9, is the façade of **Grosvenor Chambers**, once the heart of bohemian Melbourne. Painters such as Tom Roberts, Frederick McCubbin, Charles Conder and Arthur Streeton perfected their famous brand of antipodean Impressionism in these studios, and Collins Street became known for its cultural life. Sadly, most of Grosvenor Chambers was demolished in the early 1980s.

There is a veritable banquet of restaurants to choose from in this area, including **Collins Quarter**, see ④, and **The Press Club**, see ⑤.

CITY MUSEUM

At the top end of Collins Street is the **Old Treasury Building** ⑪, considered by many experts to be Australia's finest 19th-century public building. Designed in 1857 by 19-year-old John James Clark from the Public Works Department, it was completed in 1862. Today, the building houses the **City Museum**

Penny-farthing in the City Museum

(20–70 Spring Street; www.oldtreasury building.org.au; Sun–Fri 10am–4pm; charge). Here you can see exhibitions about the city's history, architecture, art and culture. Attractions include the multimedia display 'Built on Gold' in the building's basement gold vaults.

For a drink at the end of your walk, try **Bar Lourinhã**, see ⑥, a mere castanet click away in Little Collins Street.

Food and drink

① SYRACUSE

23 Bank Place; tel: 9670 1777; www.syracuserestaurant.com.au; Mon–Fri 7.30am–late, Sat 6pm–late; $$
Occupying a 19th-century bank building, Syracuse has atmosphere and style in spades. The antiques-laden dining room is gorgeous, while the Mediterranean menu tempts all tastebuds.

② CAFÉ VUE

430 Little Collins Street; tel: 9691 3899; www.vuedemonde.com.au/cafe-vue; Mon–Fri 7am–4pm; $
This café is the little sister of Vue de Monde, sharing its adherence to excellence, but it is cheaper, easier to get into and considerably less pretentious. Its pastries and croque monsieurs are justly famous.

③ HOPETOUN TEAROOMS

Shops 1 and 2, Block Arcade; tel: 9650 2777; www.hopetountearooms.com.au; Mon–Sat 8am–5pm, Sun 9am–5pm; $
Once run by the Victorian Ladies' Work Association, this tearoom has been a genteel choice since first opening its doors over a century ago.

④ COLLINS QUARTER

86-88 Collins St; tel: 9650 8500; www.collinsquarter.com; Mon–Thur 7.30am–11pm, Fri 7.30am–1am, Sat 12 noon–1 am; $$
For a post-shop drop, or to fortify yourself before hitting the streets, this cool bar and restaurant is the perfect pitstop. Head Chef Nikki Smith takes her tucker seriously, and the wine and beer list is long and lovely. There's even an open fire for those chilly Melbourne winter days.

⑤ THE PRESS CLUB

72 Flinders Street; tel: 9677 9677; www.the pressclub.com.au; Mon–Sat noon–3pm, Sun 11.30am–3pm, daily 6–10pm; $$$
In the former newspaper offices of the *Herald & Weekly Times* (hence the name), this sleek restaurant-bar is run by George Colombaris, one of Melbourne's most talented chef/ restaurateurs. The menu is modern Greek.

⑥ BAR LOURINHÃ

37 Little Collins Street; tel: 9663 7890; www.barlourinha.com.au; Mon–Thur noon–11pm, Fri noon–1am, Sat 4pm–1am; $$
This sexy bar-restaurant is a perfect spot for pre-dinner or late-night cocktails, fortified wines and a range of creative tapas.

Carrying a David Jones–branded bag on Bourke Street

BOURKE STREET

Bourke Street has a long and illustrious history as Melbourne's premier shopping and entertainment strip. There has long been a more shady side to the street, and recent years have seen sections of it move resolutely downmarket, but a number of historically and architecturally important buildings survive.

DISTANCE: 1km (0.6 mile)
TIME: A half day
START: Parliament House
END: GPO
POINTS TO NOTE: The stretch between Swanston and Elizabeth streets is closed to cars but is still open to trams, so watch where you're walking.

Crowned by the imposing edifice of Parliament House, Bourke Street can safely be described as Melbourne's main street. In the 1850s it was a crowded and rough entertainment precinct full of sly grog shops, billiard rooms, cigar divans, bowling alleys and sideshows. By the 1870s it had transformed itself into a fashionable boulevard full of shops and theatres, and was often compared with London's Oxford Street.

Generations of Melburnians have used the expression 'Busier than Bourke Street on a Saturday night', and while the street is no longer a thriving entertainment strip, it still packs a punch when it comes to retail therapy. The city's two big department stores are located here, as is the boutique shopping complex GPO and the historic Royal Arcade.

Parliament building

PARLIAMENT HOUSE

Christened as the home of the Parliament of Victoria in 1856, **Parliament House ❶** (corner Spring and Bourke streets; www.parliament.vic.gov.au; when parliament is not sitting tours leave at 9.30am, 10.30am, 11.30am, 1.30pm, 2.30pm and 3.45pm, and there's an express tour at 1pm; free) also hosted Australia's newly established Federal Parliament from 1901, only surrendering the role when legislators and the machinery of government moved to the purpose-built national capital of Canberra in 1927.

Constructed in stages, its principal spaces are the ornately decorated Legislative Council and Legislative Assembly Chambers (1856), Library (1860), Vestibule and Queen's Hall (1878–9), and Refreshment Rooms (1929). The classical façade and colonnade date from 1888 and the sweeping steps are a favoured location for everyone from newlyweds posing for photographs to political demonstrators getting their voices heard and placards seen.

Gardens
There are a number of formal gardens in the area surrounding Parliament House; these include the triangle-shaped **Parliament Gardens ❷**, the members-only Parliament House Garden and **Gordon Reserve ❸** on the corner of Macarthur Street. This picturesque reserve is home to statues of Gordon of Khartoum and the 19th-century Aus-

tralian bush poet Adam Lindsay Gordon (born 1833), whose life ended tragically in 1870 when – broke, underappreciated, demoralised and injured after a horseracing accident – he shot himself in the Melbourne suburb of Brighton. His last book, *Bush Ballads and Galloping Rhymes*, unsuccessful when it was published, is now considered a major piece of Australian literature.

The graceful fountain in the centre of the reserve was sculpted in bluestone by William Stanford (1837–80) while he was incarcerated in prison in the 1860s. Sentenced to 22 years for highway robbery and horse stealing in 1860, Stanford, a trained stonemason, developed a talent for sculpture in prison. This fountain was so highly regarded by the public that it led to a movement to commute his sentence, and he was freed in 1870.

SPRING STREET TO EXHIBITION STREET

Facing the Parliament House façade are two of the city's best-loved buildings: the Princess Theatre and Hotel Windsor. Both date from Marvellous Melbourne's heyday.

Princess Theatre
The pretty-as-a-picture **Princess Theatre ❹** was designed in the French Second Empire style, and opened in 1886 with the Australian première of Gilbert & Sullivan's *The Mikado*. Notable archi-

tectural features include the mansard towers topped with cast-iron crowns and the leadlight-adorned winter garden on the first floor. Theatre lore, backed up by anecdotes from performers and front-of-house staff, claims that there is a resident ghost here in the spectral form of a performer called Federici (real name Frederick Baker), a baritone who died here at the end of a performance of Gounod's *Faust* in March 1888 and whose spirit has never left the building.

Two of Melbourne's best café-wine bars sit comfortably in the Princess Theatre's shadow – the **City Wine Shop**, see ❶, and **The European**, see ❷ – but you will have to compete with groups of ministerial advisers from Parliament House if you decide to claim one of the outdoor tables to enjoy breakfast or a coffee. Later in the afternoon, the **Melbourne Supper Club** and its **Siglo** terrace bar above The European are wonderful spots for a drink (see page 121).

Hotel Windsor

The local equivalent of Singapore's Raffles or London's Savoy, the **Hotel Windsor** ❺ at 111 Spring Street is one of the city's major landmarks (see page 102). Opened as The Grand Coffee Palace in 1888, its owners soon gave up hope of temperance being profitable and relaunched the venue as the licensed Grand Hotel in 1897. The hotel's proximity to Parlia-

ment House meant that it was often treated as an extension of the parliamentary building – the federal constitution was drafted here in 1889 and it was the Melbourne residence of former prime minister Robert Menzies (1894–1978). Renamed The Windsor in the 1920s, its north corner wing was added between 1957–63. Renovation is scheduled to begun on the entire building, but it is uncertain whether it will meet its intended completion deadline of early 2017.

Bourke Hill's cafés

The top end of Bourke Street has long been home to a clutch of popular Italian cafés and restaurants. Many have closed in recent times, but two much-loved examples survive. **Pellegrini's** ❻, an espresso bar dating from 1955 and located at No. 66, has hardly changed in the intervening decades. It was one of the first cafés in Melbourne to possess an Italian espresso machine.

A wine bar was established at neighbouring 78–84 Bourke Street as early as 1900, but the restaurant-bar-café now known as **Grossi Florentino** ❼ dates from 1928, when the building was acquired by the Massoni family and converted into an Italian restaurant named Café Florentino. Beloved by Melbourne's establishment, the Florentino has always been split into three eating areas: a posh upstairs restaurant decorated with 16 murals depicting Renaissance Italy, a downstairs bistro, and an

Pellegrini's is the place for an espresso

atmospheric wine bar-café known as the **Cellar Bar**, see ❸.

Salvation Army Temple

Opposite Florentino, at 69 Bourke Street, is the **Salvation Army Temple** ❽, housed in a building originally erected by the Young Men's Christian Association (YMCA) and acquired by the Salvation Army in 1894. Inside is a handsome auditorium with a kauri pine-vaulted ceiling and an attic studio that was once the headquarters of the Salvation Army's Limelight Department. This small outfit designed and produced coloured lantern slides and photographs in the last decade of the 19th century. It was famous for creating the 1900 presentation *Soldiers of the Cross*, which is often described as the world's first narrative film. The department later expanded into the Limelight Film Studios, the first major film production unit in Australia. The building still functions as the Salvation Army's southern territorial headquarters.

Further down the street, on the north-eastern corner of Bourke and Exhibitions streets, is the elegant **Former London Chartered Bank**, erected in 1870–1.

EXHIBITION STREET TO SWANSTON STREET

This stretch of Bourke Street has been bastardised over the last 50 years, and few remnants of its illustrious past remain. After crossing Exhibition Street, continue downhill and you will soon see the Allans Music Building on the left, at No. 152, in a building that was once the home of the **Eastern Arcade** ❾. Look up and you will see the arcade's exotic Moorish facade, which dates from 1894.

Former Bank of NSW

Further on, over Russell Street and on the opposite side of the road at Nos 190–192, is the **Former Bank of NSW Building** ❿, which was built in 1931. The over-the-top decorative style of this building reflects the craze at that time for all things Egyptian, a phenomenon inspired by Howard Carter's 1922 discovery of Tutankhamun's tomb in the Valley of the Kings at Luxor. Note the curved top parapet formed of stylised papyrus fronds.

The stern bulk of the **Commonwealth Bank Building** ⓫ on the southern side of the street, at Nos 219–225, stands in total contrast. Built in 1940, this is the best example of an Art Deco skyscraper in the city, but it has none of the glamour of its neighbour.

BOURKE STREET MALL

The block between Swanston and Elizabeth streets has been the mercantile heart of the city since the early 20th century, when the Myer and Buckley & Nunn emporiums opened.

Queen Victoria Market

Back then, ladies from the suburbs donned hat and gloves, seized their handbags and travelled by tram to these city stores in order to enjoy a day marvelling at the modern merchandise on offer. And although the suburban mall is as common here in modern Melbourne as it is in Middle America, many locals still emulate their parents and grandparents and make regular pilgrimages into Myer and David Jones (commonly known as 'DJs') for a big day out.

David Jones

Melbourne's premier department store occupies three buildings on opposite sides of the mall. On the southern side of the mall is the **David Jones Men's Store** ⑫ (www.davidjones.com.au), formerly the G.J. Coles Department Store, a striking pink Art Deco building built between 1929–38. On the northern side is the Former **Buckley & Nunn Men's Store** ⑬, a fabulous Jazz Moderne building from 1933, featuring a façade of glossy black tiles, chrome zigzag detailing and coloured tilework details. Next to it is an elegant Edwardian building opened in 1912 as the flagship **Buckley & Nunn Emporium** ⑭. These two buildings now house the David Jones Women's Store.

Myer

There's a certain amount of truth to this store's advertising boast that 'Myer is Melbourne', as it has been a favoured shopping destination for Melburnians from as early as 1911, and the store's back story is a classic tale of an industrious immigrant achieving huge success in the greenhouse environment of Melbourne in the early 20th century. Arriving penniless from Russia in 1899, Simcha Baevski (later Sidney Myer) first found employment in a Flinders Lane clothing business, but it didn't take long for his entrepreneurial skills to emerge, and after working as a hawker he set up drapery shops in Bendigo and Melbourne before opening his magnificent self-titled emporium in the city. His store – and achievement – was so huge that locals use the saying 'more front than Myer's' to describe cheeky confidence.

The **Myer Emporium** ⑮ (www.myer.com.au) colonised large tracts of Bourke and Lonsdale streets in the 1920s and 1930s, with the construction of handsome buildings such as the Commercial Gothic structure at Nos 314–336 Bourke Street. Lauded as a 'Cathedral of Commerce' when it was opened in 1933, this building once sported a stylish Art Deco fitout, traces of which still remain. The best of these is the Myer Mural Hall, which is adorned with huge chandeliers and a mural cycle entitled *Females Through the Ages* by local artist Napier Waller.

Royal Arcade

Across the mall is the oldest surviving shopping arcade in Australia. **Royal**

The Royal Arcade

Arcade **16** is still looking spruce, courtesy of a costly and sympathetic recent restoration. Architect Charles Webb referenced the grand arcades of London and Paris in this 1869–71 confection, endowing it with a long glassed roof and installing a crown of arched windowed storerooms above the 28 shops. Original tenants included the Royal Turkish Baths (closed in 1927) and prominent clockmaker and jeweller Thomas Gaunt & Co, who made the large clock at the southern end of the arcade. The clock is guarded either side by Gog and Magog, figures of mythical British giants copied from larger effigies at London's Guildhall.

GPO

The **Former General Post Office 17** on the northeastern corner of Bourke and Elizabeth streets surrendered its philatelic and mail function in 2001 and now houses **GPO** (www.melbourne sgpo.com; Mon–Sat 10am–6pm, Fri until 8pm, Sun 11am–5pm), an upmarket shopping mall dominated by fashion retailers. Built in stages between 1861 and 1907, the building's riot of columns, elevated open arcade and visually prominent clocktower make it a true Melbourne landmark. Shops worth checking out include designer boutiques such as Larsen Jewellery and fast fashion outlets such as H&M, while there's a plethora of quality eating places and fancy watering holes to sate even the hungriest shopper's appetite – including the new Vietnamese sensation, Mama's Buoi.

Refreshment options

By this stage you are probably ready for something to eat or drink. If you are feeling peckish, turn left into Elizabeth Street and then right into Little Collins Street. Slightly up the hill on the right is tiny Gills Lane, home to the casually chic **Gills Diner**, see **4**. Alternatively, you can veer right into Elizabeth

Queen Victoria Market

A short detour north along Elizabeth Street will bring you to the historic Queen Victoria Market (corner Elizabeth and Victoria streets; www.qvm. com.au; Tue and Thur 6am–2pm, Fri 6am–5pm, Sat 6am–3pm, Sun 9am–4pm; guided tours at 10am–noon on Tue, Thur, Fri and Sat; charge for tour), where generations of Melburnians have done their weekly produce shopping. A stroll around the bustling deli hall, fruit and vegetable sheds, and fish and meat hall reinforces the fact that Australia has a range and quality of foodstuffs unparalleled in the world – if you can't find an in-season product here, you are unlikely to find it anywhere. It is always fascinating to notice the ethnicity of the market's stallholders – this has been a reflection of immigration trends in the city ever since its establishment in 1878.

GPO shopping centre on Bourke Street Mall

Street, right again into Little Bourke Street and left into dingy Driver Lane to reach **MOO** (Money Order Office, see ⑤, which is the perfect spot for a leisurely early-evening drink combined with some people-spotting.

Food and drink

① CITY WINE SHOP

159 Spring Street; tel: 9654 6657; www.citywineshop.net.au; Mon–Fri 7am–late, Sat–Sun 9am–late; $$

You can choose from a selection of 3,000 bottles here (both New and Old World), and a generous number of these are also available by the glass. The menu plays second fiddle to the wine, but still deserves an encore when it comes to both flavour and presentation. In the morning, coffee and pastries reign supreme.

② THE EUROPEAN

161 Spring Street; tel: 9654 0811; www.theeuropean.com.au; daily 7.30am–3.30am; $$$

Run by the same crew as the City Wine Shop, this elegant café-restaurant has been serving European dishes and drops for over a decade. The menu is more extensive and sophisticated than that of its neighbour, but the same laid-back European ambience features. Breakfasts are excellent and great value.

③ CELLAR BAR

80 Bourke Street; tel: 9662 1811; www.grossiflorentino.com/cellar-bar-homepage; Mon–Sat 7.30am–late; $

This classic *enoteca* has a *simpatico* menu and atmosphere. You can enjoy a simple breakfast, graze on antipasto, tuck into a rustic pasta or risotto or just relax over a coffee or glass of *vino*. The scene at the outdoor tables can be fascinating to watch.

④ GILLS DINER

Rear 360 Little Collins Street; tel: 9670 7214; www.commercialbakery.com.au; Mon–Fri noon–3pm, Tue–Sat 5–10pm; $$

One of the in-crowd's favourite city eateries, Gills Diner serves simple but delicious European-derived dishes, from a menu designed according to a locavore ethic (using locally sourced produce) paired with extremely reasonable prices. You will find it behind the Commercial Bakery.

⑤ MOO

Basement 318 Little Bourke Street; tel: 9639 3020; www.moneyorderoffice.com.au; Tue–Fri noon–3pm, Tue–Sat 6–11pm, bar Tue–Sat 5pm–late; $$$

Imagine a Baroque boudoir crossed with a London gentlemen's club and you get an idea of what Money Order Office (MOO) is like. A subterranean restaurant-bar with mood lighting and an exceptionally fine wine list, it is beloved by businessmen on the make and fashionistas from the GPO.

Celebrating Australia Day

SWANSTON STREET

Straight as an arrow and replete with history, this major boulevard is home to civic monuments and treasures from several eras, including Flinders Street Station, Federation Square, Melbourne Town Hall and the State Library of Victoria. Take a detour into Chinatown and then rinse off in the City Baths.

DISTANCE: 2.5km (1.5 miles)
TIME: A half day
START: Flinders Street Railway Station
END: Melbourne City Baths
POINTS TO NOTE: Note that the NGV Australia is closed on Mondays. Don't forget to bring your swimming things if you wish to end the walk with a dip.

Melbourne-born comedian Barry Humphries (of Dame Edna Everage fame) once quipped that Swanston Street was topped and tailed by the city's two most sacred sites: the Shrine of Remembrance and the Carlton and United Brewery. The brewery is long gone from its former home, but the shrine still stands majestic at the southern approach, and the street itself remains one of the city's best-known thoroughfares, home to many important civic and commercial buildings.

Swanston Street was an important component of Robert Hoddle's 1837 layout of the future town of Melbourne, and today it's a major tram route connecting the inner north with suburbs on the southern side of the Yarra and around Port Phillip Bay. It's blocked to cars during the day, but walk on the footpaths (sidewalks) because the road sees a steady stream of bicycles and trams. While walking, look out for street art, including the much-loved book sculpture in front of the State Library.

FLINDERS STREET RAILWAY STATION

Meeting friends 'under the clocks' at **Flinders Street Railway Station ❶** is a long and proud Melburnian tradition, so it's appropriate to start here. The banded-brick-and-render façade and copper dome of the station building have dominated the southern gateway to the city since 1910. The stained-glass windows, pressed metalwork, zinc cladding and open-air platforms overlooking the Yarra River are architecturally distinctive, but it is the famous row of clocks at the main entrance that draws most attention.

The cobblestone piazza of Fed Square

FEDERATION SQUARE

Built in 2001 to commemorate the centenary of Australia's Federation, the entertainment and cultural hub of **Federation Square** ❷ is situated opposite the station. Its dynamic and contemporary design was inspired by Melbourne's arcades and lanes, and the building is particularly distinctive when illuminated at night. Constructing the showpiece square was a massive undertaking, politically and technically, and arguments still rage over the design. It is, however, incontrovertibly Melbourne's premier public space and has shifted the whole focus of the city.

Dubbed 'Fed Square' by locals, the cobblestone piazza is surrounded by 'shards', which house restaurants, performance spaces and three high-profile cultural institutions. The square hosts major public events, including the annual Melbourne Writers' Festival. Dishing out practical information about Melbourne and Victoria, the

Melbourne Visitor Centre (www.thatsmelbourne.com.au; daily 9am–6pm) is located here, on the corner of Flinders

St Paul's   *NGV Australia*

and Swanston streets.

Between Fed Square and the Yarra River lies Birrarung Marr, a dynamic, terraced inner-city park that opened in 2002. It boasts some fantastic Melbourne-flavoured artwork – including a sound sculpture consisting of a series of computer-operated bells – and is often utilised for events. When it's not hosting a festival, this is a great spot to enjoy alfresco urban dining, taking advantage of the free barbecues provided. Birrarung Marr means 'river of mists' and 'river bank' in the language of the Wurundjeri people, who inhabited the central Melbourne area before European settlement.

Centre for the Moving Image

The **Australian Centre for the Moving Image ❸** (ACMI; www.acmi.net.au; daily 10am–6pm; charge) celebrates celluloid and other electronic arts, and has built an enthusiastic following since opening in 2002. Impressive temporary exhibitions are staged in the screen gallery, programmes of cutting-edge film are screened in two high-tech cinemas and there is even a games lab.

The Ian Potter Centre: NGV Australia

The National Gallery of Victoria has two major locations: its flagship building in St Kilda Road (see page 66) and a gallery here in the square's biggest shard. The **NGV Australia ❹** (www.ngv.vic.gov. au; Tue–Sun 10am–5pm; permanent collection free, charge for special exhibitions) houses the institution's impressive collection of Australian art. The first galleries' indigenous art ranges from traditional bark paintings to striking modern canvases. The classic colonials and Australian Impressionists come next, and, as you progress, the pieces become more modern. Look out too for a host of unique displays on Australian photography, fashion and textiles (including dresses and hats), decorative arts (homeware and accessories), sculptures and multi-media. The NGV also hosts an impressive programme of temporary exhibitions showcasing the work of contemporary Australian artists.

St Paul's Cathedral

Diagonally opposite Flinders Street Railway Station is **St Paul's Anglican Cathedral ❺**, built on the site where, in March 1836, the first religious service in the new colony was held under a great gum tree. A bluestone church built on the site in 1852 was replaced in 1891 by this Transitional Gothic building, designed by noted English ecclesiastical architect William Butterfield. The horizontally banded stone interior, organ, stained-glass windows, Venetian glass mosaics and blackwood furniture are all worth closer inspection. The cathedral's organ was imported from England and is acknowledged as the finest surviving work of T. C. Lewis, the esteemed 19th-century organ builder.

YOUNG AND JACKSON

Opposite, on the northwestern corner of Swanston and Flinders streets, is one

Melbourne Town Hall

of Australia's most famous pubs, the unassuming but splendidly sited **Young and Jackson Hotel** ❻ (www.youngandjackson.com.au; Mon–Thur 10am–midnight, Fri 10am–3am, Sat 9am–3am, Sun 9am–midnight). The three-storey bluestone building was constructed in 1853, and its upstairs dining room is home to Jules Lefebvre's beautiful 1875 nude *Chloe*, which has shocked strait-laced members of the community since being hung here in 1908.

FLINDERS LANE

Walk north and cross Flinders Lane, once the city's garment district. The names of laneways and buildings, such as Manchester Lane ('manchester' is an Australian term used for household linen or cotton goods), pay tribute to the businesses that thrived here in the 1920s to the 1960s; many of Victoria's richest family dynasties made their fortunes here. These days it features a liberal sprinkling of commercial art galleries, glam boutiques and hipster cafés.

Just off Flinders Lane are a couple of laneways – the cobbled bluestone Degraves Street and the narrow Centre Place – lined with small but vibrant eateries and bars.

If you detour left along Flinders Lane, consider stopping for breakfast or coffee at **Journal**, see ❶, or grab lunch at **Journal Canteen**, see ❷.

Head right, up the hill, to **Anna Schwartz Gallery** (185 Flinders Lane; www.annaschwartzgallery.com), home to the city's most impressive stable of contemporary artists. Next door at No. 181 is **Christine** (181 Flinders Lane; www.christineaccessories.com) beloved by fashionistas for gorgeous accessories and clothes. Near the top of Flinders Lane is fashionable bar-café-eatery **Cumulus Inc.**, see ❸.

MELBOURNE TOWN HALL

Back on Swanston Street, walk one block until you reach Collins Street. The corner here is presided over by the imposing **Melbourne Town Hall** ❼, designed in the French Second Empire style by architect Joseph Reed, who was responsible for many of Melbourne's grand 19th-century civic buildings. Completed in 1870, it was a popular venue for public meetings in its early years, and still hosts heated debates in its council chambers.

Inside the town hall is the tiny **City Gallery** (www.melbourne.vic.gov.au/citygallery; Mon 10am–2pm, Tue–Thur 11am–6pm, Fri 11am–6.30pm, Sat 10am–4pm; free), which hosts a changing programme of consistently fascinating exhibitions about Melbourne's cultural, historical and artistic life. You'll find it adjoining the **Halftix box office** (see page 20).

Opposite is the **Manchester Unity Building** ❽, featuring a soaring vertical design inspired by Chicago's Tribune Building. Constructed in 1932, at the height of the Great Depression, the 11-storey 'Goth-

Chinese Museum

ic-Deco' building was the work of noted architect Marcus Barlow. Newspapers of the time lauded it as a striking testament to the city's modernity and a vote of commercial confidence in its future.

CHINATOWN

Continue north past Bourke Street until you meet Little Bourke Street, home to Melbourne's **Chinatown** ❾. The stretch between Swanston and Springs streets is frantically busy on Sundays, when a swathe of restaurants serve *yum cha* (dim sum). Aside from food, there are also several hip bars in Chinatown that are packed cheek by jowl at weekends.

Cantonese-speaking Chinese immigrants arrived in great numbers during the 1850s, hopeful of making fortunes in the colony they described as 'New Gold Mountain'. After periods of backbreaking work on the goldfields, they came here to eat, gamble and smoke opium. Benevolent societies established premises here, including the still-functioning Sam Yup Society (now Nam Poon Shoong) at Nos 200–202, often supported by wealthy merchants and community leaders such as Low Kong Meng, who built the wedding cake–like **Sun Kum Lee Trading Company Building** at Nos 112–114 in 1887–8.

To find out more about the history of the Chinese in Melbourne, visit the **Chinese Museum** ❿ (22 Cohen Place; www. chinesemuseum.com.au; daily 10am–5pm; charge).

STATE LIBRARY OF VICTORIA

Back on Swanston Street, continue north. Cross Lonsdale Street, past the **QV Centre**, a block-sized shopping complex, and, opposite **Melbourne Central**, another cathedral of consumerism, you'll find the magnificent **State Library of Victoria** ⓫ (328 Swanston Street; www. slv.vic.gov.au; Mon–Thur 10am–9pm, Fri–Sun 10am–6pm; free).

The library was established by Lieutenant-Governor Charles Joseph La Trobe and Supreme Court judge Redmond Barry to counterbalance the upheaval of the gold rush by bringing culture, stability and an ethos of civic virtue to the colony. It was opened in stages from the mid-19th century. Don't miss the classically elegant Queen's Hall (built in 1856) and magnificent domed Reading Room (1913). Items from the library's permanent collection (including Ned Kelly's suit of armour) are on display in the Dome Galleries, while temporary exhibitions are staged in the Cowen and Keith Murdoch galleries.

In 2010, two years after Melbourne was declared a Unesco City of Literature, the **Wheeler Centre** (www.wheeler centre.com) took up residence in the library's Barry Hall. Dedicated to the advancement of writing, books and ideas, the centre hosts many events, talks and debates.

The library's excellent café, **Mr Tulk**, see ❹, is a great spot for lunch.

La Trobe Reading Room in the State Library

RMIT UNIVERSITY

North of the library, across La Trobe Street, is **RMIT University** ⑫, established in 1887 as the Working Men's College. The university has a highly regarded architecture school and has constructed a number of significant buildings and urban design interventions on campus, including Ashton Raggatt McDougall's bizarre 1992–5 addition to historic **Storey Hall** and Edmond and Corrigan's whimsical **Building 8**, a Postmodernist tour de force that dominates the university's Swanston Street frontage.

MELBOURNE CITY BATHS

Further up, across Franklin Street, are the **Melbourne City Baths** ⑬ (420 Swanston Street; tel: 9663 5888; Mon–Thur 6am–10pm, Fri 6am–8pm, Sat–Sun 8am–6pm; charge), with a public swimming pool, spa, sauna and gymnasium. Public baths were built here in 1858, but the present red-brick Edwardian building dates from 1904.

Food and drink

① JOURNAL

Shop 1, 253 Flinders Lane; tel: 9650 4399; http://journalcafe.com.au; Mon–Fri 7am–9pm, Sat–Sun 7am–6pm; $
The soaring ceilings, huge shared benches and hip vibe of this much-loved café make it a seductive pitstop at any time of the day.

② JOURNAL CANTEEN

Level 1, 253 Flinders Lane; tel: 9650 4399; http://journalcafe.com.au; Mon–Fri noon–3.45pm; $
Upstairs from Journal, this casual eatery is also known as Rosa's Kitchen in honour of its Sicilian chef. Seasonal produce dominates the daily menu and the antipasto plate is a delight, the pasta dish is always al dente and the cannoli are to die for.

③ CUMULUS INC.

45 Flinders Lane; tel: 9650 1445; www.cumulusinc.com.au; Mon–Fri 7am–11pm, Sat–Sun 8am–11pm; $$
Über-fashionable Cumulus Inc. lives up to its hype. You can wander in for a leisurely breakfast, join the local gallery set for lunch or queue for a dinner table. The kitchen is headed by one of Melbourne's best chefs, Andrew McConnell.

④ MR TULK

Corner of Swanston and La Trobe streets; tel: 8660 5700; www.mrtulk.com.au; Mon–Thur 7am–5pm, Fri 7am–9pm, Sat 9am–4pm; $
This casual café was named after Augustus Henry Tulk, the State Library's first chief librarian. Bookworms love its simple but stylish decor and keenly priced menu. Check out the daily specials.

At Toto's, Australia's first pizza restaurant

CARLTON AND PARKVILLE

This vibrant suburb north of the city centre has played host to newly arrived migrants and bohemian students since the 1850s. En route to the cafés of 'Little Italy', discover the story of Ned Kelly, relax in pretty Carlton Gardens and explore Australia's natural history at the Melbourne Museum.

DISTANCE: 4.5km (2.75 miles)
TIME: A full day
START: Old Melbourne Gaol
END: Enoteca Vino Bar
POINTS TO NOTE: Do this tour on a Saturday if you intend to watch the child-friendly play Such a Life at the Old Melbourne Gaol. Note also that you should arrange a tour in advance if you wish to visit the Trades Hall and/ or the Royal Exhibition Building. You can access Melbourne Zoo in Parkville by tram No. 55 from Elizabeth Street (Melbourne Zoo/Royal Park stop) or by train from Flinders Street Station on the Upfield or Gowrie lines (Royal Park stop).

Christened in 1852, when the *Government Gazette* advertised land for sale in 'Carlton Gardens' on the northern edge of the fledgling colonial settlement, Carlton had long been characterised by its Victorian buildings and wonderful gardens, squares, parks and reserves. Its wide tree-lined boulevards were built as extensions of William Hoddle's city grid and were soon populated by handsome buildings adorned with decorative iron lace and stone carvings.

In 1853, Melbourne's university was established on its western border, endowing the suburb with a bohemian flavour that it retains to this day. The theatres, cafés and bookshops along Lygon Street have been frequented by generations of artists, writers, students and academics, who mingled with wave upon wave of newly arrived migrants attracted by the area's cheap housing stock and proximity to the city. Today, it's the first port of call for many migrants from Africa and Asia, who live in high-rise 1960s public housing.

OLD MELBOURNE GAOL

Begin at the **Old Melbourne Gaol** ❶ (near corner of Russell and Victoria streets; www.oldmelbournegaol. com.au; daily 9.30am–5pm; charge). Fascinating and forbidding in equal measure, this bluestone gaol dates

from 1852 and is part of a large complex that comprised the prison buildings, city watch house, magistrate's court and police headquarters. The gaol was closed in 1929, superseded by a larger, more modern facility in the northern suburb of Coburg. Macabre exhibits here include death masks of well-known criminals, including the infamous bushranger Ned Kelly.

Kelly is a polarising historical figure. Some see him as a Robin Hood character, others as simply a robber and hoodlum. His deeds took place in an era when the settlement of Victoria was a rough and ready place, and they were underpinned by a sense of injustice for common people. Rightly or wrongly, he has become a great Australian icon since being executed for triple murder in 1880 here at the Old Melbourne Gaol, with the famous last words: "Such is life". The protective suit of home-made iron armour that he wore during the famous last stand against police troopers at Glenrowan is on display in the Dome Galleries at the State Library (see page 45).

There are lots of photographic panels relating to the histories and crimes of Kelly and other former inmates in the cells of the gaol. You can also see the scaffold on which Kelly and 134 other miscreants were hanged.

If you would like to learn about the life and death of Ned Kelly, the play

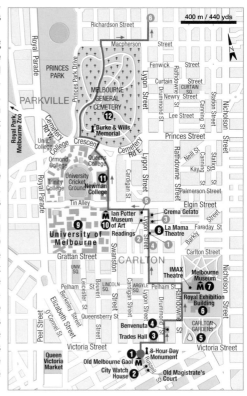

Old Melbourne Gaol

Such a Life is performed every Saturday at 12.30pm and 2pm. Included in the admission price, this one-hour performance is a hit with children and adults alike. Alternatively, take a **Ghost Tour** or a **Hangman's Night Tour** (tel: 9656 9889; times vary; charge).

The National Trust, which runs the gaol as a tourist attraction, offers a 'Crime and Justice Experience', including access to the gaol and its exhibits, plus a tour of the former **City Watch House** ❷ in which visitors have the arrest process (body searches, mugshots) explained to them by an actor masquerading as a police sergeant. During school holidays you can also visit the adjoining **Old Magistrate's Court**, a grand building where many of Victoria's most notorious criminals were convicted and sentenced for their crimes. Both tours are included in the gaol's entrance charge.

TRADES HALL

Just across from the gaol entrance, on a small traffic island, is a pink granite **monument** paying tribute to the fact that an eight-hour working day was introduced in Victoria in 1856, decades before it was attained elsewhere in the world. The demand for eight hours' labour, eight hours' recreation and eight hours' rest was the international labour movement's response to the long hours and poor working conditions that characterised the Industrial Revolution.

Diagonally across from the monument, in Carlton proper (which officially starts on the northern side of Victoria Street), is the imposing **Trades Hall** ❸ (corner Lygon and Victoria streets; tel: 9659 3511; email: info@vthc. org.au; guided tours by prior appointment Mon–Fri 9am–5pm; charge). This building dates from 1875 and it replaced an earlier, more modest structure, the world's very first trades hall – or workers' parliament – built in 1859 and frequented predominantly by stonemasons (who led the Eight-Hour Movement).

The guided tour shows you the old council chamber, murals commemorating pioneers of the local labour movement and the building's famous bullet-ridden wall, dating from an incident during WWI.

DRUMMOND STREET

Exiting Trades Hall, walk east up busy Victoria Street and take the first left onto Drummond Street, one of Carlton's premier addresses. In the late 19th and early 20th centuries a large and prosperous community of Jewish immigrants from Eastern Europe settled in the gracious two-storeyed terrace houses here and ran businesses on Lygon Street. Most of these Jewish residents moved south of the Yarra River in the 1950s, surrendering the street and suburb to a post-war wave of immigration dominated by Italians.

Carlton Gardens and the Royal Exhibition Building

To the right, look out for the over-the-top façade of **Benvenuta** ➍, a Baroque-style mansion at No. 48. Built in 1892–93 by the wealthy widow of a Jewish arms dealer and generally shady character named Henry Abrahams, this Drummond Street mansion has a colourful history, having functioned as an Italian Club, brothel and now a university hall of residence.

Reaching Queensberry Street, turn right and you will see Carlton Gardens directly ahead, dominated by the imposing facade and dome of the Royal Exhibition Building.

CARLTON GARDENS

In the early years of the settlement, visiting **Carlton Gardens** ➎ could be fraught with danger. Gangs of local boys (known as larrikins) regularly destroyed trees and flowers during rowdy games of football, and ladies enjoying a quiet perambulation were often threatened by unruly flocks of goats. All this changed during preparations for the Melbourne International Exhibition of 1880–1, when avenues of deciduous trees, huge flower beds, grand fountains, ponds and ceremonial paths were introduced. Now, each April the gardens host the wildly popular Melbourne International Flower and Garden Show.

Royal Exhibition Building

Australia has a wealth of natural landscapes and Aboriginal cultural sites on Unesco's World Heritage List, but only two built structures have been granted this honour: Sydney's Opera House and Melbourne's **Royal Exhibition Building** ➏ (9 Nicholson Street; www.museum.vic.gov.au/reb; guided tours most days at 2pm, book in advance; charge). The huge scale and classical design of this exhibition pavilion reflected the boundless energy, optimism and wealth of gold rush-era Victoria. Sited in the centre of Carlton Gardens and completed in 1880, it played host to the Melbourne International Exhibition, the Centennial International Exhibition of 1888 and the opening of Federal Parliament in 1901. The stunning interior, featuring the 1901 colour scheme and soaring ceilings, has been meticulously restored.

Melbourne Museum

Standing in stark contrast to the ornate Victorian splendour of the Royal Exhibition Building is the sleek and contemporary **Melbourne Museum** ➐ (Nicholson Street; www.museumvictoria.com.au/melbournemuseum; daily 10am–5pm; charge), designed by internationally acclaimed Melbourne-based architects Denton Corker Marshall. Located immediately north of the Royal Exhibition Building, this multimedia institution has eight galleries aimed at giving visitors an insight into Australia's natural environment, culture and history. Highlights include walking through a living rainforest and learning about local Aboriginal culture at the Bunjilaka Cultural Cen-

You will find plenty of pizza on Lygon Street

tre. The museum's most popular exhibit introduces visitors to the famous racehorse Phar Lap, a tenacious steed that won innumerable races in the midst of the Great Depression and allowed Australians to forget – if only for the length of a race – how difficult life had become.

Film fans can watch 3D movies on the world's third largest screen at the **IMAX Melbourne Museum** (www.imax melbourne.com.au).

LITTLE ITALY

Exit the museum, turn right, cross Rathdowne Street and follow Pelham Street to the city's Italian quarter, Lygon Street. This busy shopping and entertainment strip is lined with plane trees and streetside cafés. Many of these cafés are shameless tourist traps serving indifferent coffee and even worse food, but scattered among them are a number of gems.

Walk north past the touristy restaurants housed in handsome Victorian terraces and cross Grattan Street. This is the heart of Little Italy, where you can enjoy a coffee and snack at **Carlton Espresso**, see ❶, the **Lygon Food Store**, see ❷, or **Brunetti**, see ❸. If you fancy a more substantial lunch, head to **Donnini's**, see ❹, for pasta, or **Jimmy Watson's Wine Bar**, see ❺, for a plate of antipasto and a glass of excellent Australian wine.

Directly surrounding this stretch of Lygon Street you will find the city's best independent bookshop, **Readings** (www.readings.com.au) at No. 309, and the *delizioso* ice-cream parlour **Crema Gelato** at No. 342. Just to the east on Faraday Street, is the ramshackle but much-loved **La Mama Theatre** (205 Faraday Street; www.lamama.com.au) ❽, one of the few remnants of the suburb's history as the epicentre of Australia's alternative theatre scene in the 1970s.

UNIVERSITY OF MELBOURNE

Turn left at Elgin Street, walk for two blocks and you will come to the **University of Melbourne** ❾, which straddles the suburbs of Carlton and Parkville. Within its leafy grounds a number of charming Gothic-style sandstone buildings from the 19th century are scattered among stern curtain-walled 1950s blocks and unfortunate 1970s Brutalist interventions.

Ian Potter Museum of Art

There are a number of museums and galleries within the university; most impressive is the **Ian Potter Museum of Art** ❿ (corner Swanston and Elgin streets; www.art-museum.unimelb. edu.au; Tue–Fri 10am–5pm, Sat–Sun noon–5pm, closed late Dec–mid-Jan; free). The cutting-edge credentials of the gallery are heralded by Christine O'Loughlin's *Cultural Rubble* sculpture installation (1993), which adorns the main façade of the building, and

Old Quad at the University of Melbourne

the exhibition programme in the main downstairs galleries is consistently impressive. Upstairs galleries play host to changing exhibitions of items from the university's enormous art collection, including its world-class classical and archaeology collections.

Leaving the museum, walk north along College Crescent, past the main strip of university residential colleges. These include the stunningly original **Newman College** ⑪, designed by American architect Walter Burley Griffin and constructed 1915–18. Griffin and his architect wife Marion Mahony came to Australia after winning an interna-tional competition to design Australia's capital, Canberra.

MELBOURNE GENERAL CEMETERY

Crossing at the huge roundabout, you will come to the perimeter fence of the **Melbourne General Cemetery** ⑫ (www.mgc.smct.org.au; daily 9am–5pm), which has been here since 1853. Many of the first colonists are buried here, and a wander around the graves shows how short many lives were in those harsh early days. After entering through the main gate, walk through the rose garden on the right and you will eventually see the large and sombre **Burke and Wills monument**, commemorating explorers Robert O'Hara Burke and William John Wills of the Victoria Exploring Expedition, who died of exposure, exhaustion and starvation at Cooper's Creek, Queensland, in 1861, while returning from crossing the continent from south to north and mapping its hitherto unexplored interior. The ill-fated expedition had set off from nearby **Royal Park** on 20 August 1860, farewelled by a crowd of 15,000.

Returning to Entrance Avenue, proceed north. Among others, you will pass the graves of Prime Minster James Henry Scullin (1876–1953) and billiards player Walter Lindrum (1898–1960), who won the World Professional Billiards Championship in 1933 and held the title until 1950.

Melbourne Zoo

Sprawling Royal Park, west of the cemetery, is where the indigenous Wurundjeri people once camped and held huge tribal gatherings called *corroborees*. In the middle of the park is the **Melbourne Zoo** (Elliott Avenue; www.zoo.org.au/Melbourne; daily 9am–5pm; charge), one of the state's most popular tourist attractions. Opened in 1862, it is the oldest zoo in Australia and the third oldest in the world. It has a renowned conservation research programme and over 300 species of animals, all of which are housed in different bioclimatic (habitat) zones. This is an ideal place to encounter local furry friends, such as kangaroos, koalas, emus, wombats and platypuses.

Gravestones at Melbourne General Cemetery

Exiting the cemetery from the northern gate on Macpherson Street, head right to Lygon Street, then turn left and walk north for a block. Across the road is **Enoteca Vino Bar**, see ⑥, the perfect spot for an *aperitivo* or early dinner.

Food and drink

① CARLTON ESPRESSO

326 Lygon Street, Carlton; tel: 9347 8482; Mon–Sat 7am–9.30pm, Sun 8am–9pm; $
The scene here is effortlessly stylish and quintessentially Carlton. Regulars congregate at the streetside tables for excellent coffee, pizza slices and panini.

② LYGON FOOD STORE

263 Lygon Street, Carlton; tel: 9347 6279; www.lygonfoodstore.com.au; Mon–Sat 7am–5pm, Sun 8am–5pm; $
Many Melburnians had their first memorable taste of grainy Grana Padano or garlicky salami at this Melbourne institution. You can enjoy a top-quality coffee, focaccia or panini sitting indoors or outdoors, or opt to take your goodies with you.

③ BRUNETTI CAFFÈ

194–204 Faraday Street, Carlton; tel: 9347 2801; www.brunetti.com.au; Sun–Thur 6am–11pm, Fri–Sat 6am–midnight; $
Melburnians travel from every corner of the city to this *principessa* of the Lygon Street café scene to sample its peerless pastries, decadent cakes and consistently good coffee.

④ DONNINI'S RESTAURANT

320 Lygon Street, Carlton; tel: 9347 3128; www.donninis.com.au; daily noon–10pm; $$
You will feel as if you have been transported to your *nonna*'s home kitchen when you sample the excellent home-made pasta on offer at this bustling trattoria. This is comfort food Italian-style – no wonder it's perennially popular.

⑤ JIMMY WATSON'S WINE BAR

333 Lygon Street, Carlton; tel: 9347 3985; www.jimmywatsons.com; Mon 10.30am–6pm, Tue–Sat 11am–late, Sun 10.30am–3.30pm; $$
Generations of students and academics from Melbourne University have skipped afternoon classes to linger over a tipple or two at Watson's. There are tables in the rear courtyard, but most patrons prefer the minimal interior, designed by revered local architect Robin Boyd in 1962.

⑥ ENOTECA VINO BAR

920 Lygon Street, North Carlton; tel: 9389 7070; www.enoteca.com.au; Tue–Sat 9am–late, Sun 9am–4pm; $$$
Behind the ugly façade of this former neighbourhood pub is a stylish space functioning as a bar-café-restaurant-*providore*. As befits its location, the wine, food and provisions are exclusively Italian, showcasing regional varietals, classic dishes and artisan-made products.

Traffic on Brunswick Street

FITZROY

Melbourne's first suburb, this enclave on the city fringe has a down-to-earth ambience and inclusive air befitting its working-class history. The funky shopping and entertainment strips of Brunswick and Gertrude streets are a riot to explore, and some of the cool bars and quirky coffee joints are exceptional.

DISTANCE: 2.5km (1.5 miles)
TIME: A half day
START: Tram Engine House
END: Centre for Contemporary Photography
POINTS TO NOTE: After finishing this walk, you could catch tram No. 112 south along Brunswick Street to the city centre and then on to St Kilda (route 11). Alternatively, combine the tour with an afternoon in Carlton (route 4).

First subdivided in 1839, the suburb now known as Fitzroy was initially part of an area called New Town, which stretched from the northeastern corner of the City of Melbourne down towards the flats of the Yarra River at Collingwood. It was proclaimed an independent municipality in 1878.

Famous for its shabby-chic main artery, Brunswick Street, the suburb has long been the haunt of students, activists, musicians, artists and the Aboriginal community. Melbourne's major alternative arts festival, the Melbourne Fringe, was born here in 1982, and longstanding incubator of the arts, **Gertrude Contemporary Art Spaces** (200 Gertrude Street; www.gertrude.org.au; Tue–Fri 11.00–5.30pm, Sat 11.00–4.30pm), arrived on the scene the following year.

Rising rents have forced many longstanding residents to relocate north to Brunswick or west to Footscray and Yarraville, but these exiles are inevitably lured back at weekends, when they prop up the bar at favourite drinking dens, contemplate the cutting-edge at gallery openings or linger over lattes in laidback cafés.

GERTRUDE STREET

Start at the **Former Cable Tram Engine House ❶**, an elegant Italianate building on the corner of Nicholson and Gertrude streets, opposite the Royal Exhibition Building. Built in 1886–7 for the Melbourne Tramway Trust, this was an important element of Melbourne's famous cable tramway system – once

Shopping for vintage clothes at Hunter and Gatherer

the largest in the world – until 1940, when it was all electrified.

On the opposite corner, facing the Melbourne Museum, is elegant **Royal Terrace ❷**, a row of 10 three-storey bluestone terrace houses dating rom 1854. A short way east, at 64–78 Gertrude Street, is **Glass Terrace ❸**, the oldest surviving terrace building in Melbourne, built between 1854–6 for Irish-born speculator and pastoralist Hugh Glass.

Once a seedy strip frequented by drug dealers, drunks and other down-at-heel Fitzrovians, Gertrude Street has reinvented itself in recent years. Boutiques and ateliers, such as **Cottage Industry** (67 Gertrude Street; www.cottageindustrystore.

blogspot.co.uk) and **Crumpler** (corner of Gertrude and Smith streets; www.crumpler.com/au/crumpler-fitzroy), showcase wares made by local artisans and designers, while stylish bars and eateries attract both locals and visitors. The best include top-notch tapas bar **Añada** (197 Gertrude Street; www.anada.com.au), **Gertrude Street Enoteca**, see ❶, and **Ladro** (224 Gertrude Street; tel: 9510 2233; www.ladro.com.au), home to the city's best pizzas.

BRUNSWICK STREET

Proceed north into Brunswick Street and head past the huge public-housing estate called Atherton Gardens, with its Russian Matryoshka Dolls sculpture (by Bronwen Gray). Further along, past the popular Malaysian restaurant **Blue Chillies**, see ❷, is the street's signature building at Nos 236–253, on the corner of Greeves Street. Built in 1888, the building's polychrome brickwork, central tower and corner turret are familiar to all Melburnians, who refer to it as the **Black Cat Building ❹**, after **Blackcat** (252 Brunswick Street; www.blackcatfitzroy.com; daily 10am-1am) the casual venue – café by day, lively bar by night – that occupies the corner shopfront, which has become is a Fitzroy institution.

The stretch between Greeves and Westgarth streets is where most of Brunswick Street's action plays out. Popu-

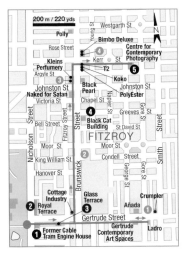

Watering hole on Brunswick Street

lar watering holes include the retro-cosy **Black Pearl** (304 Brunswick Street; www.blackpearlbar.com.au), grungy **Bimbo Deluxe** (376 Brunswick Street; www.bimbodeluxe.com.au), wickedly good **Naked for Satan** (285 Brunswick Street; www.nakedforsatan.com.au) and vaguely louche **Polly** (401 Brunswick Street; www.pollybar.com.au). For lunch or coffee, the perennially popular choices are **Marios**, see ❸ and **Babka**, see ❹.

Look out for pavement mosaics and shopfront decorations as you walk – all have been created by local artists.

CONTEMPORARY PHOTOGRAPHY CENTRE

Turn east into Kerr Street and walk to the George Street junction. Here you'll find the **Centre for Contemporary Photography** ❺ (CCP; 404 George Street; www.ccp.org.au; Wed–Fri 11am–6pm, Sat–Sun noon–5pm; free), a purpose-designed space showcasing changing exhibitions of photography and video art. Even after dark you can enjoy artwork, courtesy of the Projection Window.

Food and drink

❶ GERTRUDE STREET ENOTECA

229 Gertrude Street; tel: 9415 8262; www.gertrudestreetenoteca.com; Mon–Fri 8am–10pm, Sat 10am–10pm; $$

They take food and wine seriously at this tiny café-cum-wine-bar, and local gastronomes return the favour. The food menu is limited, with a strong emphasis on seasonal produce and simple execution, but there's an impressive choice of wines by the glass. The coffee is excellent too, particularly when accompanied by biscuits and cake made daily on the premises.

❷ BLUE CHILLIES

182 Brunswick Street; tel: 9417 0071; www.bluechillies.com.au; daily noon–2.30pm, Mon–Thur 6–10.30pm, Fri–Sat until 11pm, Sun until 10pm; $$

The curry *laksa* (noodle soup) here is justly famous, but alternatives such as beef *rendang* and *char kway teow* (Malaysian fried rice noodles) are equally delicious.

❸ MARIOS

303 Brunswick Street; tel: 9417 3343; www.marioscafe.com.au; daily 7am–11pm; $

There is an over-abundance of cafés on Brunswick Street, but this one reigns supreme for three reasons: great coffee, all-day breakfasts and fast and friendly service.

❹ BABKA

358 Brunswick Street; tel: 9416 0091; Tue–Sun 7am–7pm; $

Breakfast and Babka is a match made in heaven (with recipes from Russia). Breads and pastries fresh from the oven are served with home-made jam. Queuing for a table is de rigueur.

Detail on a house on Powlett Street

EAST MELBOURNE

Elegant East Melbourne is in a class of its own. Its proximity to the city centre, Victorian-era streetscapes and genteel atmosphere make it an address many Melburnians aspire to. This route explores historic Eastern Hill and Fitzroy Gardens.

DISTANCE: 1.25km (0.75 mile)
TIME: 3 hours
START: Orica House
END: Fitzroy Gardens
POINTS TO NOTE: Orica House is located between Carlton Gardens and Parliament House. This short walk could easily be combined with Bourke Street (route 2), Carlton (route 4) or Fitzroy (route 5). If you decide to visit the Johnston Collection, it is essential to book at least one day in advance of your preferred visiting time.

When the Anglican Bishop of Melbourne and his wife set up house in East Melbourne in 1853, they were the first well-connected members of society to call the suburb home. Their bluestone house, 'Bishopscourt', survives to this day on the corner of Clarendon and Gipps streets, surrounded by a score of gracious Victorian townhouses occupied by surgeons, barristers, investment bankers and arts professionals, many of whom walk to their workplaces through the historic Fitzroy Gardens.

There's serious money here, but little ostentation, making it a classy contrast to the gilded suburbs south of the Yarra.

ORICA HOUSE

Start at **Orica House ❶** on the corner of Albert and Nicholson streets, formerly known as ICI House, designed by local architectural firm Bates Smart McCutcheon and completed in 1958. This was the first building to break the 132ft (40.2m) height limit then applied to all city buildings, and was the tallest building in Australia until 1961. A Modernist masterpiece, it features the steel frame and curtain-wall glass so beloved by European and American architects of the post-war period, but it horrified many local critics at the time.

EASTERN HILL

Walking east along Albert Street, you'll pass the distinctive red-and-white **Salvation Army Printing Works** at Nos 500–502 and the **City of Melbourne Synagogue** at Nos 494–498. The syn-

Fire Services Museum

agogue was built between 1877–83, and its Renaissance Revival façade stands in almost frivolous contrast to the stern classical portico of the **Former Baptist Church** (at Nos 486–492), which dates from 1863.

A short detour left (north) up Gisbourne Street will bring you to the **Eastern Hill Fire Station ❷** on the corner of Victoria Parade, built as a headquarters for the newly established Metropolitan Fire Brigade and opened in 1893. Sited at the highest point of the city, its 52-metre (171ft) tower once commanded panoramic views over Melbourne, perfect for fire spotting.

The station now houses the **Fire Services Museum** (39 Gisbourne Street; www.fsmv.net.au; Thur–Fri 9am–3pm, Sun 10am–4pm; charge), with displays of fire engines and fire-fighting equipment that young children adore.

The foundation stone for the pretty Anglican church of **St Peter's Eastern Hill ❸** on the southwestern corner of Albert and Gisbourne streets was laid by Lieutenant-Governor Charles Joseph La Trobe on 18 June 1846. Parts of the church date from 1848, making it one of the few pre-gold rush buildings in central Melbourne. It's been modified many times, most recently in 1945,

when a stained-glass window by artist Napier Waller was added.

Across Gisborne Street, sitting in a 2-hectare (5-acre) site gifted to the Catholic Church between 1848–53, is the Gothic Revival **St Patrick's Cathedral ❹**. Erected in stages from 1858 to 1940, the scale of Architect William Wardell's design is magnificent. The stained glass was produced by workshops in Munich and Birmingham.

With the 19th century Catholic population of Melbourne predominantly Irish, the cathedral was named for Ireland's patron saint, and a statue of Daniel O'Connell (1775–1847), 'The Liberator' of Irish Catholics, stands in the grounds. A Jesuit grammar school once stood behind the cathedral, but the bluestone tower in the southeastern corner is all that remains. In its place is the **Catholic Archdiocese of**

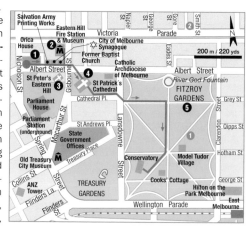

Cooks' Cottage, Fitzroy Gardens

Melbourne headquarters, which features a circular courtyard and tranquil water pools fronting Albert Street.

FITZROY GARDENS

Cross Lansdowne Street to the charming **Fitzroy Gardens** ❺, laid out in the 1850s and still boasting original elm trees, formal paths, sweeping lawns, statuary and a number of structures, some more felicitous than others. The Spanish Mission–style **Conservatory** is particularly attractive. Also here is **Cooks' Cottage** (www.cookscottage.com.au; daily 9am–5pm; charge), the home of Captain James Cook's parents. Originally built in 1755, it was transported here from Yorkshire in 1933 and, technically, is the oldest building in Australia.

In the centre of the gardens is **The Pavilion Fitzroy Gardens**, see ❶, where you can enjoy a coffee or tea at the end of your walk. Alternatively, walk north out of the gardens, going past the **River God Fountain**, and head to **Amaretto Trattoria**, see ❷, for some lovely down-to-earth Italian tucker.

Johnston Collection

The Johnston Collection (www.johnston collection.org) is a house museum on Hotham Street, to the east of Fitzroy Gardens. The legacy of antiques dealer William Robert Johnston, the collection occupies Fairhall, a Georgian-style house dating from 1860. The museum opened in 1986, showcasing Johnston's extraordinary collection of Georgian, Regency and Louis XV furniture and decorative arts. Because the Johnston Collection is located in a residential street (one of Melbourne's grandest), it doesn't have a standard museum permit. To visit, you must book a place on one of the three tours that operate every weekday (10am, noon and 2.15pm); you'll be collected by minibus from the foyer of the Hilton on the Park Hotel on Wellington Parade, at the southeastern corner of Fitzroy Gardens.

Food and drink

❶ THE PAVILION FITZROY GARDENS

Fitzroy Gardens, Wellington Parade; tel: 9417 2544; www.thepavilion fitzroygardens.com.au; daily 9am–4pm; $
This glass pavilion nestled in the gardens is a popular spot to enjoy a cup of coffee or tea. Indoors has floor to ceiling windows or you can sit on the terrace.

❷ AMARETTO TRATORIA

205 Victoria Parade; tel: 9417 5169; www.amarettobistro.com.au; Mon–Fri noon–3pm and 6–11pm, Sat 5–11pm; $–$$
East Melbourne has few restaurants and cafés, but this unassuming little gem serves great Italian cuisine with zero pretention. The friendly owner/chef is passionate about his food. You can BYO wine.

Rowing on the Yarra

THE YARRA AND DOCKLANDS

Its murky appearance has led to the Yarra being described as a river flowing upside down, but the indigenous Wurundjeri people refer to it more poetically as Birrarung, the River of Mist. This waterside walk takes in world-class sports arenas, memorable Southbank views and high-class restaurants.

DISTANCE: 6.5km (4 miles)
TIME: A full day
START: Melbourne Cricket Ground (MCG)
END: NewQuay, Docklands
POINTS TO NOTE: To get to the MCG, you can walk east from the city centre, take a train to Jolimont Station (Epping or Hurstbridge lines), take tram No. 48 or 75 travelling east along Flinders Street (Jolimont Station stop 11) or take the No. 70 tram from Flinders Street (Melbourne Park stop 7C). To return, catch the free City Circle tram from Harbour Esplanade.

The Yarra

At first glance, the Yarra River may seem to lack visual appeal and strategic importance, but an exploration of its central section is an introduction to the soul of the city. Icons dot its banks, boats skim its surface and umpteen Melburnians enjoy its sporting and recreational amenities at weekends and on summer evenings.

In 1835, John Batman's identification of fresh water above falls 10km (6 miles) from the river's mouth determined the location of the settlement that would become Melbourne. Later, Robert Hoddle aligned his grid for the city's streets with its course. Ever since, the river has been a topographic landmark, demarcating the northern and southern sides of town. With the development of the Docklands and South Wharf precincts at the western edge of the city centre, the Yarra draws together the leafy residential east and the still-industrial west.

Travelling on the Yarra is an excellent way to connect with the city. **Melbourne Water Taxis** (www.melbournewatertaxis.com.au; daily 9am–midnight; charge) offers on-demand services up and down the Yarra, into the Docklands and over the bay to Williamstown. It also runs a regular service between Southgate and Melbourne Park/MCG when concerts and sporting events are on.

Cycling is a great way to explore the riverbanks. **Rentabike @ Federation Square** (www.rentabike.net.au;

AFL game at the MCG

daily 10am–5pm) at Federation Wharf (under Princes Bridge on the Federation Square side of the river) rents bikes for adults and children by the hour or day.

MELBOURNE CRICKET GROUND

Australians have a unique attitude towards sport, supporting teams and individual players with an evangelical fervour rarely exhibited in the nation's churches. Although each state has its signature stadium, only one has a sporting shrine – and that's Victoria's **Melbourne Cricket Ground ❶** (MCG; Brunton Avenue; www.mcg.org. au). Known to Melburnians as 'the G', this massive structure stages international cricket matches and Australia's hugely popular home-grown football code, Australian ('Aussie') Rules. It was also the main venue for the 1956 Olympic Games.

Aussie rules
Australia's first football match was played in 1858 by cricketers looking for an off-season sport. The game thrived on the rivalry and class differences between the suburbs and the fierce pride of players and fans. Although the class differences may have diminished and the teams' ties to suburbs have become tenuous, the power and the passion of the code remains. Weekend footy continues to be an intrinsic part of life for millions of Melburnians, and

for many players the pinnacle of their career is an appearance at the G, preferably in a Grand Final (see page 22).

Test cricket
Fans of cricket are similarly devoted. Cricket has been played at the MCG since 1853, and the ground hosted the first-ever test match in 1877. The Boxing Day Test at the G is world-famous, and a summer afternoon spent in the stands watching the Australian test or one-day sides strut their stuff is a right of passage.

Stadium tours
The MCG is one of the largest stadiums in the world, with a capacity of 100,000. One-hour guided tours depart from Gate 3 of the Olympic Stand most non-event days between 10am and 3pm.

National Sports Museum
It's possible to purchase a ticket for the stadium tour that includes entrance to the **National Sports Museum** (www. nsm.org.au; daily 10am–5pm; charge), which is located within the MCG's Olympic Stand. The museum complex houses a collection of sports artefacts, covering 20 sporting codes.

The museum incorporates Australia's Game (tracing the history of Australian rules football), Melbourne Cricket Club Museum, and Champions: Thoroughbred Racing Gallery (formerly Australian Racing Museum), plus temporary exhibition areas.

Auditorium of the State Theatre

MELBOURNE AND OLYMPIC PARKS

Cross the footbridge over Brunton Avenue on the southern side of the stadium and you'll find yourself in another sporting precinct – **Melbourne & Olympic Parks** ❷ (www.mopt.com.au). Here, the **Rod Laver Arena** and **Hisense Arena** host the Australian Tennis Open (see page 23) and concerts. Melbourne United basketball team lives in Hisense Arena and the Collingwood Football Club (aka the Magpies) is based at the **Westpac Centre**, with a training ground on the site of the now-demolished Olympic Park.

Situated within this sports precinct too is the stunning **AAMI Park** (www.aamip-ark.com.au), built for rectangular sports. Opened in 2010, it's the home ground of A-League football (soccer) teams Melbourne City FC and Melbourne Victory FC, rugby league team Melbourne Storm and rugby union team, the Melbourne Rebels. It features a cutting-edge bioframe design with a geodesic dome roof, which covers the seating area and is designed to allow over 30,000 spectators an unobstructed view.

BIRRARUNG MARR

From the Rod Laver Arena, walk north past the tennis courts and cross the footbridge over Batman Avenue to enter **Birrarung Marr** ❸, the first major area of parkland to be created in the city for

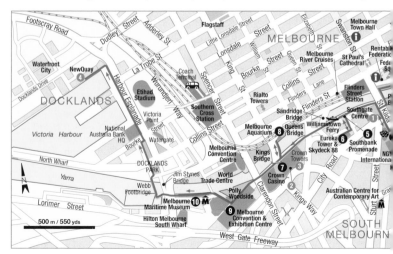

National Sports Museum

Federation Bells in Birrarung Marr

over a century. This 8.3 hectare (20-acre) park features free barbecues, indigenous flora, river views, a children's playground and the **Federation Bells**, a set of computer-controlled bells that play specially commissioned pieces on a daily basis.

ARTS CENTRE

Follow the river past Federation Square (see page 42) and cross to the other bank via Princes Bridge. On the western side of St Kilda Road is one of the city's major visual landmarks, the distinctive latticed spire of the **Arts Centre ❹** (100 St Kilda Road; www.theartscentre.com. au). The state's pre-eminent performing arts complex, it comprises the State

Theatre, Hamer Hall (principal venue for the Melbourne Symphony Orchestra), Playhouse Theatre and Fairfax Studio.

The Arts Centre houses the Performing Arts Collection, over 200,000 items relating to the history of performing arts in Australia, including personal memorabilia from artists. A regular exhibition programme showcases items from the collection, many of which have been donated by the artists. Past subjects have included Kylie Minogue, Barry Humphries (aka Dame Edna Everage) and Nick Cave.

The Spiegeltent

A popular, albeit transient, attraction is the Spiegeltent, a travelling entertainment salon that appears in the forecourt during the Melbourne International Arts Festival (see page 20). Dating from the early 20th century, there are only a handful of these flamboyantly decorated European 'mirror tents' left. During the festival, it hosts cabaret, live music and artists' talks.

SOUTHBANK

Leaving the Arts Centre, walk to **Southbank ❺**, a wide paved promenade along the river, backed by the Southgate Centre. There are plenty of cafés and restaurants here including the popular dim sum restaurant **Red Emperor**, see ❶. The main attraction, however, is the promenade itself. After sunset, the view of the city skyline is spiked with the spire of St Paul's Cathedral, the dome of

Skydeck 88 in the Eureka Tower

Flinders Street Station and a constellation of glowing office towers. Make sure you check out the sculptures on the Sandridge Bridge as you walk by.

Behind the Southgate development (accessed via Southgate Avenue) is **Eureka Tower** ❻, the tallest building in Melbourne and the highest residential tower in the world. Vertiginous views can be enjoyed from **Skydeck 88** (Riverside Quay; www.eurekalookout.com. au; daily 10am–10pm; charge) on – you guessed it – the building's 88th floor.

CROWN CASINO

Backtrack to Southbank, continue walking west, past the departure point for ferries to Williamstown (see page 84) and cross Queensbridge Street to arrive at **Crown Casino** ❼ (www.crowncasino. com.au; daily 24 hrs). The complex presents a relatively boring face to the water – there's only a modicum of Vegas-style glitz and glamour here – but the futuristic chimney stacks that line the riverbank do shoot flames into the air every hour after dusk, and inside it has a cinema complex and a smorgasbord of restaurants, including **Rockpool Bar & Grill**, see ❷, and **Bistro Guillaume**, see ❸.

MELBOURNE AQUARIUM

Opposite the Casino, accessed via Kings Bridge, is the **Melbourne Aquarium** ❽ (corner King and William streets; www.melbourneaquarium.com.au; daily 9.30am–6pm, Jan until 9pm; charge), where an impressive collection of sea creatures occupy specially designed tanks, including a 2.2 million-litre (500,000 gallon) Oceanarium where intrepid visitors can dive with sharks (while wide-eyed schoolkids press their noses to the glass, some of them urging the sharks to take a nibble).

SOUTH WHARF

Returning to the southern bank of the Yarra, you'll see the **Melbourne Exhibition Centre** on the right. It is known to locals as Jeff's Shed after Jeff Kennett, the former premier of Victoria whose government funded its construction.

Behind the shed, in the area known as South Wharf, is the **Melbourne Convention Centre** ❾ (www.mcec. com.au). Opened in 2009, it is the only 6-Star Green-Star environmentally rated convention centre in the world. Within this vicinity is a retail and dining promenade, office tower, Hilton Melbourne South Wharf and the **Melbourne Maritime Museum** ❿ (www.pollywoodside.com.au; daily 9.30am–5pm; charge), a showcase for the beautifully restored three-masted iron barque Polly Woodside, launched in Belfast in 1885.

DOCKLANDS

Cross to Docklands via the Jim Stynes Footbridge – Melbourne's newest

View of the CBD and Princes Bridge

bridge, opened in 2014 and named after a much-loved Irishman who became an Aussie Rules legend for Melbourne Football Club before passing away from cancer, aged just 45, in 2012. When the Victorian State Government gave the go-ahead for a private-sector redevelopment of Melbourne's Docklands, it insisted 1 per cent of the development costs be dedicated to an urban art programme. This led to 29 public artworks being commissioned for the precinct. Most reflect the themes of water, indigenous history, and the city's industrial and maritime past – but there's at least one cow up a tree. Look out for it while walking through **Docklands Park**, keeping Etihad Stadium on your right. After about 15 minutes you'll come to **NewQuay**, a mix of residential towers and restaurants overlooking the harbour. The area has struggled somewhat to live up to expectations, and some high-profile eateries have shut their doors in recent years, but **Cargo**, see ❹, is an excellent spot for a beer and a feed.

Food and drink

❶ RED EMPEROR

Level 2, Southgate Arts & Leisure Precinct, Southbank; tel: 9699 4170; www.red emperor.com.au; Mon–Sat noon–3pm, Sun 11am–4pm; $$$

This highly popular Chinese restaurant offers great views of the city and Yarra River. It's known for excellent service and some of the best dim sum and seafood dishes created by experienced masterchefs.

❷ ROCKPOOL BAR & GRILL

Crown Casino; tel: 8648 1900; www.rockpool.com/rockpoolbarandgrill melbourne; Sun–Fri noon–3pm and 6–11pm, Sat 6–11pm; $$$$

Sydney's Neil Perry caused a few local feathers to fly when he announced his intention to open here in Melbourne, but all was forgiven as soon as his inspired take on comfort cooking was sampled. Make sure your credit card has leverage.

❸ BISTRO GUILLAUME

Crown Casino; tel: 9292 4751; www.bistro guillaume.com.au; daily noon–3pm and 6pm–late; $$$

This modern French bistro with stylish surrounds serves classic dishes such as leg of duck confit and steak frites.

❹ CARGO

55a New Quay Promenade; tel: 9670 0999; daily 7am–late; $$

Good, solid, well-priced fare from coffee and brioche-based breakfasts through to burgers and (craft) beer in the evening. Plenty of menu options, a cracking location and friendly professional service.

Water feature in the Pioneer Women's Memorial Gardens

KINGS DOMAIN AND ROYAL BOTANIC GARDENS

In Melbourne, some define themselves as sophisticated south-of-the-river types and others are staunchly north-of-the-river, but both groups cherish this green oasis to the immediate east of the city's grand boulevard, St Kilda Road.

DISTANCE: 2.75km (1.75 miles)
TIME: A half day
START: NGV International
END: Royal Botanic Gardens
POINTS TO NOTE: To join a tour of Government House, you will need to book at least seven days in advance. To return to the city centre at the end of the walk, catch the No. 8 tram west along Domain Road.

Looking at St Kilda Road today, it's hard to believe it was once called Baxter's Track, named after a man who used it as a stock route between the southern banks of the Yarra River and the seaside settlement of St Kilda. After the first bridge over the river was constructed in 1845, approximately 40 hectares (100 acres) of land to the east of the track was set aside for a botanical reserve (now the Royal Botanic Gardens), and the track itself was upgraded to a tree-lined road. Wealthy colonists purchased land lots along it; they hoped that the presence of the bluestone Victoria Bar-

racks (1856) would protect them from the bushrangers who occasionally held up parties of travellers heading south.

After the construction of Government House in 1876, St Kilda Road's status as the colony's great ceremonial route was confirmed. Today, the road and the Kings Domain and Royal Botanic Gardens on its eastern edge are among the city's most popular tourism and leisure attractions.

NGV INTERNATIONAL

Begin the tour to the south of Federation Square and the Yarra, where **NGV International ❶** (180 St Kilda Road; www.ngv.vic.gov.au; Wed–Mon 10am–5pm; permanent collection free, charge for some temporary exhibitions) sits on the corner of St Kilda Road and Southbank Boulevard. Of Melbourne's many cutting-edge cultural institutions, the National Gallery of Victoria (NGV) is the one held most dear by the arts establishment. Established in the 1860s, it remains the pre-eminent art gallery in the country.

Originally housed in the State Library Building in Swanston Street, the NGV's col-

lection moved here in 1968. The aesthetic merits of Roy Grounds' fortress-like design were hotly debated at that time, but the building has subsequently become one of the most cherished in the state, particularly loved for its sculpture-adorned moat, entrance water wall and Len French-de-signed Great Hall ceiling.

NGV International showcases world-class collections of decorative arts, Asian and Oceanic art, 18th- and 19th-century English painting and European Old Masters. Don't miss Tiepolo's *The Banquet of Cleopatra* (1743–4), Andy Warhol's *Self portrait No.9*, or Picasso's *Weeping Woman* (1937). In August 1986, this Picasso's masterpiece was stolen by a group calling itself the Australian Cultural Terrorists. The thieves demanded the establishment of a A$25,000 art prize as a ransom, but the NGV refused to meet their demand. Eventually an anonymous tip-off led to the undamaged canvas being recovered in a railway station locker, but the culprits were never identified.

KINGS DOMAIN

Cross St Kilda Road in front of the gallery and walk to **Kings Domain ❷**, a large public park on the southern side of Linlithgow Avenue. Once part of the formal grounds of Government House, the area was redesigned,

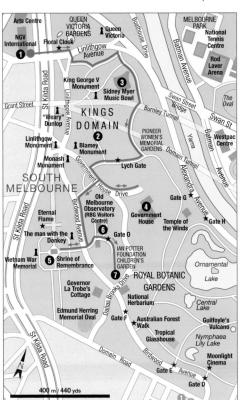

The Shrine of Remembrance

replanted and opened to the public in 1935 to commemorate Melbourne's centenary.

Ahead, on the park's northern edge, is the 1959-built **Sidney Myer Music Bowl ❸**. The design for this outdoor music and entertainment venue was inspired by the Hollywood Bowl and is significant for melding revolutionary engineering techniques with an organic structural form that sits perfectly in the landscape of the Domain.

Government House

Head south into the park past the **Pioneer Women's Memorial Gardens**. You will soon see the landmark square tower of **Government House ❹** (www.governor.vic.gov.au/government-house; tours Feb–mid-Dec Mon and Thur, book at least seven days in advance; charge), the home of Victoria's governors since 1876. Modelled on Queen Victoria's Osborne House on the Isle of Wight, this Italianate pile has a huge ballroom that accommodates 2,000 guests and a number of smaller staterooms. Guided tours of the building also take in nearby **La Trobe's Cottage**, a modest prefabricated building that was shipped here from England in 1840 and functioned as the colony's first government house.

The Shrine of Remembrance

Cross from Government House east to Birdwood Avenue and walk south. Government House may be the largest building in Kings Domain, but it's overshadowed in the hearts and minds of Melburnians by the **Shrine of Remembrance ❺** (www.shrine.org.au; daily 10am–5pm, guided tours 11am and 2pm; free), built to honour the 114,000 Australians who served in WWI and to memorialise the 19,000 who died. A third of Melbourne's population is estimated to have attended the opening ceremony on Armistice Day, 1934.

The shrine's impressive subterranean visitor centre provides educational and exhibition spaces, and facilitates entrance into the original building, which has a design inspired by the Parthenon at Athens and the Mausoleum at Halicarnassus. Inside, the focal point is a black marble stone of remembrance inscribed with the words 'Greater love hath no man'. On 11 November at 11am, the time when the hostilities of World War I ceased, a ray of light shines through an aperture in the roof and rests on the word 'love'.

The forecourt and its eternal flame were added in 1954 to recognise service in World War II, while the Remembrance Garden commemorates later conflicts.

ROYAL BOTANIC GARDENS

Cross Birdwood Avenue to the **Old Melbourne Observatory ❻**, now the visitor centre for the city's magnificent **Royal Botanic Gardens** (www.rbg.vic.gov.au; daily Nov–Mar 7.30am–8.30pm, Apr and Sept–Oct 7.30am–6pm, May–Aug 7.30am–5.30pm; free). Land was set aside here for public gardens in 1846,

Royal Botanic Gardens

but the design seen now – with sweeping lawns, meandering paths, rocky outcrops and an ornamental lake at its centre – was created in 1879–1909 by the director William Guilfoyle.

The gardens contain a vast range of plants from all over the world, laid out in their respective climatic zones. You can see rainforest giants (on the Australian Forest Walk), desert cacti, Alpine wild flowers and temperate shrubs. No one knew how foreign trees and plants would survive when planting first began, but the first director, Ferdinand von Mueller, instigated a programme of plant classification, identification and conservation in the gardens' herbarium in 1857, which continues to this day, making this one of the most important botanical gardens in the world.

Watching a film under the stars at the **Moonlight Cinema** (www.moonlight.com. au/melbourne) in the Royal Botanic Gardens on a summer night is a Melbourne tradition. Theatrical performances are also staged on the lawns around the lake - check the entertainment listings in the 'EG' section of Friday's Age (www.theage. com.au/entertainment)

Children's Garden

Those travelling with children shouldn't miss the interactive **Ian Potter Foundation Children's Garden** ❼ (Wed–Sun 10am–sunset except for two months in winter, daily during school holidays; free). Here the aim is for kids to learn about nature while having fun picking flowers, getting their hands dirty, scrambling around in overgrown plant tunnels and discovering what's croaking in the pond.

If you have provisions with you, favourite spots for an alfresco feast are the lake, with its fountain, ducks and swans; and the Temple of the Winds, a classical folly overlooking the Yarra River. Alternatives include the café at the visitor centre or the kiosk near the lake. For a more substantial meal, try **The Botanical**, see ❶, or **Bacash**, see ❷, in nearby Domain Road.

Food and drink

❶ THE BOTANICAL

169 Domain Road; tel: 9820 7888; www.thebotanical.com.au; Mon–Fri 7am–11pm, Sat–Sun 8am–11pm; $$$$
Located along a leafy street near the Royal Botanic Gardens, this place draws regulars with its plush setting, modern creations and fine wines. There is also a chef's menu, designed by Lionel Abello, with wines to match selection.

❷ BACASH

175 Domain Road; tel: 9866 3566; www.bacash.com.au; Mon–Fri noon–3pm and 6pm–late, Sat 6pm–late; $$$
This is one of Melbourne's best seafood restaurants, a temple to all things piscatorial. Owner and chef Michael Bacash lets the quality of his produce speak for itself, eschewing fussy sauces or overly clever combinations.

Chapel Street shops

PRAHRAN, SOUTH YARRA AND TOORAK

These upmarket suburbs on the southern bank of the Yarra are beloved by the local bling brigade. This route saunters along hip Greville Street, chichi Chapel Street and the gilded thoroughfare of Toorak Road, concluding at colonial Como House.

DISTANCE: 3.25km (2 miles)
TIME: A half day (more if serious shopping is on the agenda)
START: Prahran Railway Station
END: Como Historic House and Garden
POINTS TO NOTE: The easiest way to get to Prahran Station is to catch the Sandringham Line train from Flinders Street Station. To return to the city centre from Como House, catch the No. 8 tram travelling west along Toorak Road.

The streets of these inner southern suburbs are endowed with dramatically different characters. Busy Chapel Street is noisy with smart boutiques and cafés frequented by a young trendy crowd, whereas the ritzy retail strip of Toorak Road has an older, moneyed vibe. Greville Street and Commercial Road are different again, one carrying the retail baggage of a hippie past and the other being noticeably LGBT. Visitors come here to shop, show off, cavort among the café culture and party like crazy.

The first subdivision of land in this part of town was in 1840, with large Crown allotments being sold in what was to become the City of Prahran. These were in turn divided into desirable estates on the hills and far less desirable blocks of land in the swampy lower-lying areas. The different land prices inevitably led to the municipality developing two distinct demographics – upper class and working class – as well as a wide array of building styles. Initially accessed via a punt across the Yarra (hence the name Punt Road for the main traffic artery from the north), Prahran boomed in the 1880s after a cable tram service was introduced in 1888. In 1887 the municipality was divided into four wards: Windsor, Prahran, Toorak and South Yarra, with Chapel Street linking them all.

WINDSOR

Once the province of brickworks, quarries and market gardens, the suburb of Windsor may have lost its solid working-class credentials, but it retains

Prahran Town Hall   *Bangles in a boutique*

a rough-around-the-edges charm beloved by students and arty types. The shops, restaurants and nightclubs at the southern end of Chapel Street are an endearing mix of grunge and glamour – favourites include the **Chapel Street Bazaar** (Nos 217–223), home to vintage furniture, objets d'art and collectors' items, as well as popular nightclub **Revolver Upstairs** at No. 229 (see page 123).

PRAHRAN

Our route proper begins in Prahran, pronounced 'P'ran'. Chapel Street is always bumper-to-bumper, so the best way to arrive is by train. From **Prahran Railway Station ❶**, walk east into **Greville Street**. Once a hippie mecca, this strip is now known for its funky clothing boutiques and casual cafés. At the end of the street is the stolid **Prahran Town Hall ❷**, a Victorian Italianate pile dating from 1861.

Prahran Market

From the Town Hall corner, turn left into Chapel Street, walk north to the major cross street of Commercial Road. Located here is the popular **Prahran Market ❸** (Nos 163–165; www.prahranmarket.com.au; Tue, Thur and Sat dawn–5pm, Fri dawn–6pm, Sun 10am–3pm), dating from 1891. One of the two best markets in the city (along with Queen Victoria Market), it sells top-quality fresh produce and has a western annexe that hosts a food hall and gourmet kitchenware/grocery stores such as **The Essential Ingredient** (www.theessential

Necklaces in a Toorak jewellery shop

ingredient.com.au). Foodies can also check out the cooking school here.

On Tuesday, Thursday and Sunday from 9.30am to 12.30pm, Australian Farmyard Friends gives kids a chance to get up close to farm animals such as lambs, goats and rabbits.

Chapel Street boutiques

After backtracking to Chapel Street, continue north and you'll come to one of Melbourne's best boutique belts, home to Australian fashion labels such as Alannah Hill (533 Chapel Street; http://shop.alannahhill.com.au). Also in this stretch is **AY Oriental Tea House**, see ❶, a popular all-day *yum cha* joint.

SOUTH YARRA

Arriving at the major intersection of Chapel Street and Toorak Road, you have two choices. If you're keen to indulge in some more shopping, veer west up the gentle incline to South Yarra Village. The boutiques here sell international designer goods and are guaranteed to give your credit card a serious workout. But if you're after lunch, there is also an impressive array of cafés and restaurants to choose from along this strip, such as **Two Birds One Stone**, see ❷, and **France-Soir**, see ❸. Alternatively, you can choose to walk east, past the Como Centre, a huge office and retail development, to Toorak, Melbourne's equivalent of Beverly Hills or Bel-Air.

TOORAK

Although a close neighbour, staid Toorak is worlds away from sybaritic South Yarra. Home to more than a quorum of Melbourne's establishment, it oozes conservatism, wealth and power. Here, credit cards are platinum, European sedans are a dime a dozen and blonde highlights are mandatory.

A walk around the streets showcases myriad mansions dating from the late 19th and 20th centuries, but all pale into insignificance when compared with the magnificent National Trust–run property Como House, accessed by heading east on Toorak Road and, after about seven blocks, turning left into Williams Road and walking one block north.

Como House

Como Historic House and Garden ❹ (corner of Williams Road and Lechlade Avenue; www.comohouse.com.au; daily 10am–4pm; charge) started life in 1847 as a single-storey villa constructed from bricks made using Yarra River mud. Nestled amid 20 hectares (50 acres) of bushland, it was a one-hour journey by horse, carriage and punt to and from the city, where the original owner, Edward Eyre Williams, worked as a barrister. Sold to a Scotsman, John Brown, in 1853, the original building was soon adorned with a second storey, extensive outbuildings and a formal garden designed by William Sangster, one of the colony's best-known gardeners. This orgy of expenditure was to have an unfortunate outcome, with

Como Historic House

Brown suffering financial reverses and being forced to sell the property in 1864.

The new owners were Charles and Caroline Armytage, wealthy pastoralists from the Western District, who used Como as their Melbourne base. Renowned for their entertaining, they added a ballroom and billiard room and furnished the house with furniture and objets d'art purchased from Europe. After they died, the house was inherited by their three unmarried daughters, who subdivided the land in 1911 and 1921, and then sold the house, furnishings and garden to the National Trust in 1959.

Enthusiastic and knowledgeable volunteer guides take visitors on a guided tour of the house and outbuildings, but the 2-hectare (5-acre) garden can be explored unaccompanied. The sweeping views down to the Yarra are impressive, and the vegetable garden, sloping lawns and flower walks are lovely.

After you have admired everything, do as the colonial gentry did and indulge in afternoon tea at the **Stables of Como Café**, see ④, in the estate's grounds.

Food and drink

① AY ORIENTAL TEA HOUSE

455 Chapel Street, South Yarra; tel: 9826 0168; www.orientalteahouse.com.au; Sun–Wed 10am–1pm, Thur 10am–11pm, Fri–Sat 10am–11.30pm; $

Giving a South Yarra twist to the traditional Chinese tea house, this stylish emporium tempts with fragrant teas, tasty *yum cha* morsels and custard buns.

② TWO BIRDS ONE STONE

12 Claremont Street; tel: 9827 1228; www.twobirdsonestonecafe.com.au; Mon–Fri 7am–4pm, Sat–Sun 8am–4pm; $

Top coffee, friendly service and amazing breakfasts and brunches with gluten-free options available. The menu sparkles with a range of made-on-the-premises delights, including homemade crumpets.

③ FRANCE-SOIR

11 Toorak Road, South Yarra; tel: 9866 8569; www.france-soir.com.au; daily noon–3pm and 6pm–midnight; $$$

For classic French dishes served with a soupçon of sophistication go no further than this Melbourne institution. The steak béarnaise is a favourite, as is the *magret de canard* (whole duck breast) and steak tartare.

④ STABLES OF COMO CAFÉ

Como Historic House and Garden, South Yarra; tel: 9827 6886; www.thestablesof como.com.au; Mon–Sat 9am–5pm, Sun 10am–5pm; $

Tuck into a delicious Devonshire cream tea in this delightful café, or pick up a lovingly made picnic – complete with Aggie's lemonade scones, jam, cream and the option of a champagne bucket – and find a sunny spot in the grounds of Como House.

SOUTH MELBOURNE
AND ALBERT PARK

Residents of this upmarket enclave rarely stray too far from home and are content to enjoy its chic cafés and impressive sporting facilities. Having tasted their lifestyles, conclude with culture at the Australian Centre for Contemporary Art.

DISTANCE: 7.25km (4.5 miles)
TIME: A full day
START: South Melbourne Market
END: Australian Centre for Contemporary Art
POINTS TO NOTE: To reach the starting point for this route, catch the No. 96 tram from Bourke Street in the city centre and get off at South Melbourne station (stop No. 127). To return to the city, catch tram No. 1 from outside the Australian Centre of Contemporary Art on Sturt Street (stop No. 18).

Strategically located between Port Phillip Bay and the city centre, these inner southern suburbs are the favoured stamping grounds of Melbourne's advertising and media professionals and have a sophisticated sheen to prove it.

It's a far cry from the district's humble beginnings, when canvas tents were erected on the southern side of the Yarra River to house temporarily the overflow of immigrants landing in the colony en route to the fabled goldfields of central Victoria. Originally known as Emerald Hill, South Melbourne became an independent municipality in 1855 and soon outgrew its boundaries, extending into the surrounding districts of Port Melbourne, Albert Park and Middle Park.

From 1890, cable trams rattled up and down the thriving commercial hub of Clarendon Street, linking the city centre with the desirable residential pocket of Albert Park and the popular sea baths at Kerferd Road Beach.

SOUTH MELBOURNE

Alight from the tram and, immediately ahead, you will see **South Melbourne Market** ❶ (corner Coventry and Cecil streets; www.southmelbournemarket.com.au; Wed and Sat–Sun 8am–4pm, Fri 8am–5pm). Locals have been shopping here since 1867, and the jumble of produce stands, food stalls and hawkers is endearingly eclectic, selling everything from sausages to saucepans.

Jogging by Albert Park Lake

The market boasts an amazing offering of ready-to-munch food and tables to eat it at, but the surrounding streets are home to a cluster of cafés specialising in brunch – try walking east along Coventry Street, claim a seat at **GAS**, see ❶, and soak up its laidback latte-driven ambience.

Stroll along Coventry Street and you'll soon reach a wide boulevard lined with Victorian-era buildings. Every Melbourne suburb has its equivalent of an English high street, and here Clarendon Street claims this honour. Its shopping options are nothing to get excited about (try Coventry Street instead), but its historic shopfronts complete with iron verandas attest to the suburb's long mercantile history.

South Melbourne Town Hall

Turn right and walk to Bank Street; the **South Melbourne Town Hall** ❷ is on the crest of a small hill to the west. Built in 1879–80 on the highest point in the suburb (the 'Emerald Hill' that gave the suburb its original name), this handsome building in

Port Melbourne beach

the classical style has an imposing clock tower and giant Corinthian-order portico.

Back on Clarendon Street, continue walking until you reach the next intersection, Park Street. Cross the street and look back towards the city to admire the façade of the **Patros Knitting Mills Building ❸** on the northern side of the street at Nos 256–264. This two-storey terrace, featuring Gothic-style windows and a square tower, was built in the 1880s.

ALBERT PARK

Walk west along Park Street, cross Ferrars Street, follow the tram tracks and turn south into Montague Street. Here you'll find yourself in one of Melbourne's most prestigious residential precincts, **St Vincent Place ❹**. Designed in 1854–5 to resemble square developments in London, it's dominated by central gardens and huge buildings like **Rochester Terrace** at Nos 33–51, dating from 1879.

Albert Park Village

Continue walking south to Bridport Street, the heart of Albert Park Village. The scene here is moneyed professional. Weekend brunch is an air-kissing free-for-all, but the weekday lunch scene is more sedate. Admire the designer frocks and accessories in **Husk** (123 Dundas Place; www.husk.com.au; Mon–Fri 10am–6pm, Sat 10am–5.30pm, Sun 10am–5pm) or browse in the excellent **Avenue Bookstore** (127 Dundas Place; www.avenue-bookstore.com.au; daily 9am–6pm). Of

the many handsome buildings in this precinct, the four-storeyed **Biltmore** (152 Bridport Street) is the most imposing , with the most interesting history. In the late 19th century approximately 60 grand coffee palaces were built around Melbourne by the temperance movement to provide alcohol-free alternatives to the city's numerous rowdy public houses. The Albert Park Coffee Palace, built in 1887–9 at 152 Bridport Street, was one of these. It was turned into residential apartments in the 1990s.

South Melbourne Beach

Follow the tramline and, at 2–36 Victoria Avenue, you'll pass the heritage-listed **Albert Park Primary School**, which dates from 1874. At the end of the street is a modest strip of sand known as **South Melbourne/Middle Park Beach**. Look right and in the distance you will see Station Pier, the terminal for cruise ships and the Spirit of Tasmania ferries that ply the waters of Bass Strait between Melbourne and Devonport in Tasmania.

Turn left and walk along Beaconsfield Parade until you reach **Kerferd Road Pier ❺**, built in 1887–9. In the late 19th century Melburnians flocked here at weekends, to enjoy the swimming baths (since demolished), promenade on the pier and socialise at Hotel Victoria at the corner of Kerferd Road and Beaconsfield Parade. After a spell as a restaurant, this heritage building was converted into private apartments. Luckily you can still get

ACCA   *Black swan on Albert Park Lake*

a great feed at **Stavros**, see ❷, not far from Beaconsfield Parade.

Albert Park and lake

Turn left into Kerferd Road and walk until you reach **Albert Park** ❻, a huge recreational reserve set around a lake where outdoorsy Melburnians walk, jog, bird-watch, picnic, sail, kick footballs and practise their golf drive. It is also home to the Australian Formula One Grand Prix, held in March each year.

The park's most popular attraction is the **Melbourne Sports & Aquatic Centre** ❼ (MSAC; Aughtie Drive; www.msac.com.au; Mon–Fri 5.30am–10pm, Sat–Sun 7am–8pm; charge), which has Olympic-sized indoor and outdoor swimming pools, plus a wave pool, sauna, spa and steam room. Overlooking the lake is **The Point**, see ❸.

AUSTRALIAN CENTRE FOR CONTEMPORARY ART

Leave the reserve at the Albert Road exit and walk down Clarendon Street until you reach Park Street. From this corner, catch the No. 1 tram heading towards East Coburg and alight at stop No. 18 in front of the huge rusted-steel monolith that houses the **Australian Centre for Contemporary Art** ❽ (ACCA; 111 Sturt Street; www.accaonline.org.au; Tue and Thurs–Sun 10am–5pm, Wed 10am–8pm; free), where five exhibitions annually showcase Australian and international contemporary art.

Food and drink

❶ GAS

253 Coventry Street, South Melbourne; tel: 9690 0217; www.gaseatery.com.au; Mon–Fri 8am–6pm, Sat–Sun 8am–5pm; $

Ladies who lunch share tables with ad execs and market traders at this exemplar of South Melbourne's chic café culture. Regulars swear by the tasty Middle Eastern and Mediterranean dishes including lamb kofta and Spanish omelettes.

❷ STAVROS

183 Victoria Avenue, Albert Park; tel: 9699 5618; www.stavrostavern.com.au; Tue–Sun 6–10pm; $

This popular Greek tavern has been around since 1979. Dig into hearty moussaka and chargrilled octopus, complemented by fine wines. On Fridays and Saturdays, enjoy live Greek music alongside some dancing and plate smashing.

❸ THE POINT

Aquatic Drive, Albert Park Lake; tel: 9682 5566; www.thepointalbertpark.com.au; daily noon–3pm and 6pm–late; $$$

As a nation, Australia has more than its fair share of cattle stations. Strange, then, that good steakhouses are few and far between. This sophisticated example is consistently commended for the quality and cooking of its beef.

Jogging along St Kilda beach

ST KILDA AND BALACLAVA

Although geographically close, these two suburbs are poles apart in every other respect. St Kilda has a sybaritic seaside–resort ambience first acquired in the 1850s, while sensible Balaclava is home to a large chunk of the city's Orthodox Jewish population and has always had a solidly suburban air.

DISTANCE: 4.25km (2.75 miles)
TIME: A full day
START: Jewish Museum of Australia
END: Balaclava Railway Station
POINTS TO NOTE: To reach the Jewish Museum of Australia from the city centre, catch tram No. 67 or No. 3 from Swanston Street and get off at stop No. 32; the museum is a two-minute walk to the east. To return to the city, catch a train from Balaclava Station to Flinders Street Station or hop on tram No. 16 or No. 3 to Melbourne University via Swanston Street. To visit Ripponlea near Elsternwick, catch the Sandringham line train from Balaclava Station one stop to Ripponlea Station. Alternatively, catch tram No. 67 to Carnegie from Balaclava Station and alight at stop No. 42. To return to the city, catch the train to Flinders Street or the tram to Swanston Street.

St Kilda

The bayside suburb of St Kilda has always been Melbourne's favourite playground. A train line from the city centre to the bay was built as early as 1857, and many of the colony's earliest entrepreneurs and professionals followed it, building mansions on St Kilda Hill where they could escape the smells, noise and occasional pestilence of the city centre.

When cable trams reached the suburb in 1888, less affluent Melburnians flocked here at weekends and holidays to enjoy a dip in the sea baths, a promenade along the pier or a stroll around the pleasure gardens. The more sedentary among them opted to watch the moving pictures at the Palais, enjoy a mild flirtation at the Palais de Danse or ride the carousel at Luna Park. Many day-trippers enjoyed their weekends here so much that they chose to move into one of the profusion of boarding houses that operated from 1890, or rent an apartment in one of the modern blocks constructed in the first decades of the 20th century.

The existence of these apartment blocks means that the suburb has long been the most densely built and pop-

Suburb insignia   *Café in Acland Street*

ulated area of Melbourne. Today, it is home to young professionals and arty types, with backpackers and blow-ins from every corner of the city descending on Fitzroy and Acland streets at weekends to enjoy its cafés, bars, restaurants and slightly seedy nocturnal street life.

Balaclava

In contrast, Balaclava has retained the amenities and atmosphere of a staid and predominantly Jewish suburb, with kosher butchers, haberdashers and bagel shops managing to hold their own against a creeping influx of trendy cafés, wine bars and boutiques.

JEWISH MUSEUM OF AUSTRALIA

Start at the **Jewish Museum of Australia** ❶ (26 Alma Road; www.jewish museum.com.au; Tue–Thur 10am–4pm, Sun 10am–5pm; charge). The multimedia exhibits at this community museum give visitors a crash course in Jewish history and culture, as well as documenting the history of Jews in Australia.

Visitors can also take a guided tour of the nearby 1,000-seat **St Kilda Hebrew Congregation Synagogue** at 10–12 Charnwood Grove (tours Tue–Thur 12.30pm, Sun 12.30pm and 3pm); it was built in 1927 on the

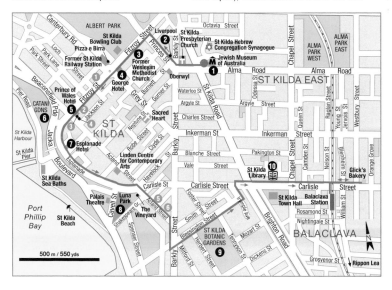

Tram to St Kilda

site of a previous synagogue dating from 1872.

ST KILDA HILL

Leaving the museum, head west, cross the busy highway and head towards Barkly Street. On the corner is the bluestone **St Kilda Presbyterian Church**, with its distinctive witch-hat tower. Directly opposite the church, on the northwestern corner is **Liverpool ❷**, a mansion built in 1888 by Nathaniel Levi (1830–1908), the first Jewish member of the Parliament of Victoria.

In this immediate area, which is known as St Kilda Hill, you will notice other historically significant mansions, including **Oberwyl** on the corner of Princes and Burnett streets. This Regency-style mansion has functioned as a private residence, exclusive girls' school and the headquarters of the Victorian Alliance Française. Continuing northwest down Princes Street, you will soon come to the suburb's most famous strip.

FITZROY STREET

Turning left into Fitzroy Street, you will soon pass a pretty bluestone church building covered in creeping vine. This is the **Former Wesleyan Methodist Church ❸**, built in 1857–8 to host services for the prosperous colonists who resided in St Kilda in its early days. On the other side of the street, a bit further on, is the **St Kilda Bowling Club**, a local institution. Hosting games of bowls, quoits, croquet and skittles, the clubhouse was established on this site in 1865, and the present building dates from 1926. Next door is the **Former St Kilda Railway Station**, a rare example of an intact Victorian-era railway station. Trains no longer run to St Kilda, and the station now functions as a tram stop and restaurant cluster, with venues including **Pizza e Birra** (see page 119).

Opposite the station is the **George Hotel ❹**, a grand resort-style hotel on the corner of Grey Street dating from 1857. In the late 20th century it became famous as a live-music venue of unparalleled grunginess (one of the venues where Nick Cave and the Bad Seeds started their careers). The basement bar at the **George** (www.thegeorgehotelstkilda.com.au) still hosts live music and is open late, but upstairs the building now houses fashionable apartments.

St Kilda has long had a reputation for crime, prostitution and drugs – first earned in the 1940s, when servicemen on leave flocked here looking for red-light action, an era documented by local artist Albert Tucker in his acclaimed series of paintings, *Images of Modern Evil* – and despite the recent gentrification of the suburb, areas such as Grey Street still host street-based sex workers and

At the Bowling Club

attendant shady characters. It isn't a place to linger late at night.

Lunch options

Although Fitzroy Street is full of restaurants and cafés, with **Mirka at Tolarno Hotel**, see ❶, and **Café Di Stasio**, see ❷ worth a try.

On the corner of Acland Street is the **Prince of Wales Hotel** ❺. Once infamous for its rough front bar, it was extensively renovated in the 1990s, and while the bar remains impressively bohemian, the venue is also home to a boutique hotel (see page 109), restaurant and spa retreat. Turn left off Fitzroy Street at the Prince corner to encounter a raft of popular eateries including **Il Fornaio**, see ❸, and **Lau's Family Kitchen**, see ❹.

Catani Gardens

At the western end of the street are the historic **Catani Gardens** ❻, a 6-hectare (15-acre) reserve on the foreshore of St Kilda Beach. The landscaping and plantings here date from the late 1920s, and the most distinctive feature is the many tapering palm trees lining the paths.

UPPER ESPLANADE

Continue along Fitzroy Street and follow the tramline along the Upper Esplanade. Apartments in the 1930s blocks along this stretch are hot property, with sunset views over the bay and blissfully briny breezes. The best-known building, though, is the **Esplanade Hotel** ❼ (aka the 'Espy'), an endearingly egalitarian watering hole and regularly raucous live-music venue. St Kilda has always had a vibrant live-music scene and many local musicians have sung tributes to its charms. The best-known of these is perhaps singer-songwriter Paul Kelly, whose song *From St Kilda to King's Cross* is an ode to Melbourne's colourful suburb.

LUNA PARK

As you walk towards the end of the Esplanade you'll spot the twin cupolas of the **Palais Theatre**, a former picture palace dating from 1927, now a concert venue. You may also hear shrill screams issuing from its neighbour, **Luna Park** ❽ (18 Lower Esplanade; www.lunapark.com.au; hours vary, check website; free entry, ride ticket charge), built in 1912 and long famous as the home of the exhilarating Scenic Railway rollercoaster. Consider taking a spin on the funpark's gorgeous carousel (with 68 hand painted horses), which was built in America in 1913 and installed here in 1923.

ACLAND STREET

At the roundabout, enter the tree-lined shopping strip of Acland Street, known for a belt-busting block of shops selling decadent European-style cakes.

Palais Theatre

Take cake and coffee at **Monarch Cake Shop**, see ⑤, enjoy a leisurely lunch with the locals at ever-popular **Cicciolina**, see ⑥, or sink a beer or two at **The Vineyard** (71a Acland Street; www.thevineyard.com.au) an unpretentious bar with outdoor seating where backpackers, bohemians and the occasional businessman rub shoulders till late.

ST KILDA BOTANIC GARDENS

Walk to the end of Acland Street, veer right into Barkly Street and then turn left at Blessington Street. Here you'll find the

---

Rippon Lea

Built by Frederick Sargood, a businessman and politician who made his fortune selling soft goods on the Victorian goldfields, the Romanesque-style Rippon Lea (192 Hotham Street, Elsternwick; www.ripponleaestate.com.au; Sept–Apr daily 10am–5pm, May–Aug Thur–Sun 10am–4pm; charge) is one of the few remaining great 19th-century suburban estates in Melbourne. Building commenced in 1868 and continued until 1897, with an Art Deco ballroom and swimming pool added by subsequent owners in 1939. The wonderful garden features a lake, waterfalls, mature trees, fernery, a hill and grotto, all of which were designed or planted between 1868 and the 1880s.

St Kilda Botanic Gardens ⑨ (corner Blessington and Tennyson streets; www.portphillip.vic.gov.au/st_kilda_botanic.htm; daily sunrise–sunset; free), established in 1861. There's a subtropical rainforest conservatory here, plus a giant chessboard and an ornamental pond. The gardens are particularly wonderful November–April, when the Alistair Clark Memorial Rose Garden is in full bloom.

CARLISLE STREET

Leave the gardens and continue walking east along Blessington Street. Cross the manic intersection of St Kilda Road/Brighton Road and enter Carlisle Street, home to the **St Kilda Town Hall**. Look out for the **St Kilda Library** ⑩ on the left-hand side of street, complete with a witty facade resembling a giant book.

The shopping strip to the east of the library and Town Hall is notable for being the favoured patch of Melbourne's Jewish community, and is home to bagel shops, kosher butchers and stores specialising in accoutrements such as menorahs. The most popular store here is **Glick's Bakery** (330 Carlisle Street; www.glicks.com.au), which sells boiled bagels, cinnamon rolls and other tasty treats.

From Glick's Bakery, backtrack two streets to **Balaclava Railway Station**, where you can catch a train back to the city or continue on to the National Trust property Rippon Lea (see box).

Luna Park entrance | At a cake shop on Acland Street

Food and drink

1 MIRKA AT TOLARNO HOTEL

42 Fitzroy Street, St Kilda;
www.mirkatolarnohotel.com; tel: 9525
3088; daily noon–late; $$$
French-born artist Mirka Mora and her
art-dealer husband Georges ran a legendary
bohemian restaurant here in the 1960s,
and Mirka's charming murals have survived
a recent, very classy, renovation. The menu
created by renowned chef Guy Grossi
features perfectly executed French and
Italian dishes.

2 CAFÉ DI STASIO

31 Fitzroy Street, St Kilda; tel: 9525 3999;
www.distasio.com.au; daily noon–3pm and
6–11pm; $$$
Restaurateur Ronnie Di Stasio has endowed
his self-named restaurant with a unique
sense of theatricality as well as a faithful
adherence to unfussy Italian cuisine. The
wine list is just as impressive (Di Stasio
has his own vineyard in the Yarra Valley).
The well-priced set-lunch menu of two
courses and a glass of wine is a Melbourne
institution. Book ahead.

3 IL FORNAIO

2 Acland Street, St Kilda; tel: 9534 2922;
www.ilfornaio.net.au; daily Mon–Fri
7am–5pm, Sat–Sun 8am–5pm; $
The industrial-chic decor may scream 21st-
century St Kilda, but the delectable breads,
pastries and cakes served at this bakery-café

are classically European. It claims to serve
Melbourne's best lattes.

4 LAU'S FAMILY KITCHEN

4 Acland Street, St Kilda; tel: 8598 9880;
www.lauskitchen.com.au; Sun–Fri noon–
3pm, 6–10pm, Sat 6–10pm; $$
Forget chandeliers, tuxedoed waiters or
huge numbered menus – what's on show
here is freshly prepared and consummately
presented Cantonese cuisine served in
fashionably minimalist surroundings.

5 MONARCH CAKE SHOP

103 Acland Street, St Kilda; tel: 9534
2972; www.monarchcakes.com.au; daily
7.30am–9pm; $
This outlet was established by a Polish
émigré in 1934 and eventually bought by
current owner Gideon Markham in 1996.
The bestseller here is the rich chocolate
kooglhoupf, a large ring-shaped cake
made according to the shop's original
recipe. Grab a table by the sidewalk and
tuck into some good old-fashioned cakes
with coffee.

6 CICCIOLINA

130 Acland Street, St Kilda; tel: 9525 3333;
www.cicciolinastkilda.com.au; Mon–Sat
noon–11pm, Sun noon–10pm; $$
How do we love thee, Cicciolina? Let us
count the ways. We love your modern
seasonal menu, your reasonable prices and
your welcoming rear bar. But, most of all, we
love your boisterous atmosphere.

Yachts moored in front of apartments in Williamstown

WILLIAMSTOWN

Melburnians flock to the waterside suburb of Williamstown to enjoy weekend promenades along Nelson Place and admire the city skyline across the bay. This relaxed route showcases the suburb's village atmosphere, maritime heritage and historic streetscapes.

DISTANCE: Walk: 5km (3.25 miles)

TIME: A half day (full day if you visit Scienceworks as well)

START: Gem Pier

END: Williamstown Beach

POINTS TO NOTE: Melbourne River Cruises (www.melbcruises.com.au) depart from Berth 5, Lower Promenade, Southgate, between 10.30am and 2.30pm (May–Sept) or 3.30pm (Oct–Apr) every day (about an hour); sailings increase in summer and at weekends. The last return service leaves Williamstown at 3.30pm. Williamstown Ferries (www.williamstownferries.com. au) run from Berth 1 daily (10.30am and 4.30pm, last return from Gem Pier 5.30pm). Williamstown Bay and River Cruises (www.mlm.com.au/work/bay rivercruises) operate a year-round, fair-weather-only service on weekends and public holidays between St Kilda and Williamstown. You can also reach Williamstown by train from Southern Cross or Flinders Street railway stations.

Much of Williamstown's rich maritime history remains, giving the suburb a historical resonance appreciated by salty seadogs and landlubbers alike.

History of Williamstown

John Batman and the first settlers of what would become the colony of Victoria arrived by sailing ship in 1835 from Van Diemen's Land, (now Tasmania) alighting at Point Gellibrand with 500 sheep and 500 cattle. In 1837 the newborn settlement was divided into two towns: Melbourne, named after British Prime Minister William Lamb (Lord Melbourne), and Williamstown, which took its moniker from King William IV.

The deep harbour at Point Gellibrand was chosen for the colony's main port, and a lighthouse and landing pier were built. The huge Alfred Graving Dock, home to a colonial navy that was a forerunner of the Royal Australian Navy, followed in 1874.

Unusually, Victoria was founded by free settlers rather than convicts, but it had an imported convict population and, in the 1850s, five rotting prison hulks were moored off Point Gellibrand to

Inside HMAS Castlemaine

house these miscreants, who were put to work mining bluestone from a nearby quarry, which was used to construct many of the suburb's first buildings.

But, in 1887 engineers finished work on the Coode Canal. By cutting out a long, looping bend in the Yarra where the river wound through the West Melbourne swamp, the canal brought ships right into the heart of Melbourne, bypassing Williamstown. Gradually the once-important port was relegated to the status of a backwater. Fortunately, its grand 19th-century commercial buildings, residences and boat-building industries were retained.

GEM PIER

The most enjoyable way to get to Williamstown is to take a ferry from Southgate, just across the Yarra from Flinders Street Station. If you are interested in hands-on science, ask to stop en route at **Scienceworks** (2 Booker Street, Spotswood; www. museumvictoria.com.au/scienceworks; daily 10am–4.30pm; charge), an interac-

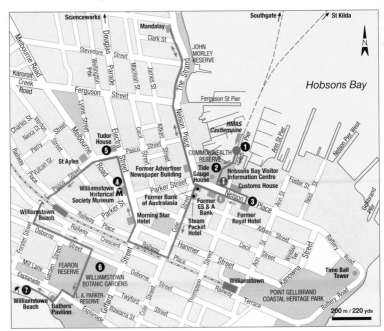

Nelson Place

tive museum that aims to make science an adventure for the visitor. The museum incorporates the old **Spotswood Pumping Station**, home to huge engines that once pumped the sewage and associated odours from 'Marvellous Smellbourne' as it was once facetiously called, as well as a state-of-the-art **planetarium**.

When continuing to Williamstown, alight at **Gem Pier** ❶. Williamstown's first jetty was built here between 1839–47, and the pier has subsequently been demolished and rebuilt three times – most recently in 1992.

HMAS Castlemaine

Locally built **HMAS *Castlemaine*** (www.hmascastlemaine.org.au; Sat–Sun 10am–4pm; charge), a 1941 minesweeper that saw active service in New Guinea and Northern Australia during World War II, is moored here and is a big hit with kids, who love clambering aboard and seeing the wheel, compasses and radar screen at the helm.

COMMONWEALTH RESERVE

Walk from the pier towards **Commonwealth Reserve** ❷. Early immigrants were carried from sailing ships on the shoulders of burly seamen and dumped onto unprepossessing mudflats lined with saltbush and a scattering of modest buildings. The mudflats were replaced between 1880–1930 by this harbourside park, created using earth dredged from shipping channels.

In the reserve today you'll find a **Tide Gauge House**, which once protected a valuable tide gauge imported from England, and the helpful **Hobsons Bay Visitor Information Centre** (www.visithobsonsbay.com.au; daily 9am–5pm). The popular Williamstown Craft Market (www.williamstowncraftmarket.com.au) is held here on the third Sunday of each month from 10am–4pm

NELSON PLACE

During the 1850s gold rush, thousands of diggers flocked to Victoria. Ships crammed into Hobsons Bay, a new pier was built, and service industries, including shipwrights, banks, boarding houses and pubs, sprang up along the harbour in **Nelson Place** ❸. Surviving buildings from this period include the handsome **Customs House** (1873–5); the **Former Royal Hotel** (1890) at No. 85; the Gothic-style **Former ES&A Bank** (1873) at No. 139; the **Former Advertiser Newspaper Building** (1885–8) at Nos 205–206, one-time home of the still-in-circulation *Williamstown Advertiser*; and the **Former Bank of Australasia** (1876) on the corner of Cole Street.

Residents made wealthy by these local industries built impressive residences along the western extension of Nelson Place, which was given the genteel name of The Strand. Look out for **Mandalay** at no. 24, a colonial Georgian residence built in 1858 for a ship chandler named Captain William Probert.

Fresh fish and chips   *Williamstown Marina*

The cafés, restaurants and pubs along Nelson Place are notable for their historic premises rather than their produce. If you're peckish, a good option is fish and chips from **Williamstown Mussels Fish and Chippery**, see ❶.

HISTORIC PUBS AND HOUSES

From Nelson Place, turn south into Cole Street. On the first corner, you'll see the **Steam Packet Hotel** (11–13 Cole Street; www.steampackethotel.com) built in 1863 to replace an earlier inn. Continue south and turn right into Railway Place to find another historic pub, the 1889 **Morning Star Hotel** (3 Electra Street; tel: 9397 6082).

Williamstown Historical Society Museum
Nearby is the **Williamstown Historical Society Museum** ❹ (5 Electra Street; www.williamstownhistsoc.org.au; Sun 2–5pm or by appointment; free), housed in a Mechanics' Institute building dating from 1860. The museum details the suburb's maritime history and houses other exhibits illustrating life here from the 1840s.

At the corner of Electra and Pasco streets is elegant **Tudor House** ❺, built in 1884 for prominent politician and lawyer William Henry Roberts. Turn left into Pasco Street to see handsome **St Ayles** at No. 72, which dates from 1891.

Keep on walking and you will reach the **Williamstown Beach Railway Station**, a stop on the oldest government railway line in Victoria which, from 1857, carried passengers from Spencer Street in central Melbourne to Williamstown Pier.

BOTANIC GARDENS AND BEACH

Walk under the railway line and turn left into Osborne Street until you reach the **Williamstown Botanic Gardens** ❻, a 4-hectare (10-acre) reserve established in 1860 and remodelled in 1905. Saunter past the rows of tall palm trees standing sentinel and then through the pine-treed L.A. Parker Reserve, from where you can admire the striking 1930s Bathers' Pavilion, now a café and kiosk, on **Williamstown Beach** ❼, one of Melbourne's most attractive suburban beaches.

Take the ferry or train back from the Williamstown Beach Railway Station.

Food and drink

❶ **WILLIAMSTOWN MUSSELS FISH AND CHIPPERY**

129 Nelson Place; tel: 9399 9961; winter Mon 11.30am–7.30pm, Wed–Sun 11.30am–9pm, summer Sun–Mon, Wed–Thur 11.30am–9pm, Fri–Sat 11.30am–late; $

Forget the overpriced and underwhelming fare on offer in the eateries along Nelson Place. Instead, order fish and chips from this popular takeaway outlet and claim a bench in Commonwealth Reserve.

A Yarra Valley wine estate

YARRA VALLEY

This postcard-pretty region on Melbourne's eastern edge is perfect for a day trip. At weekends there are nearly as many cars here as there are cows, with Melburnians descending en masse to soak up the valley's views and varietals.

DISTANCE: 50km (31 miles) from central Melbourne to Yering Station, 34km (21 miles) for this route and 55km (34 miles) back to Melbourne
TIME: A full day
START: Yering Station
END: Domaine Chandon
POINTS TO NOTE: You'll need to rent a car for this route. From central Melbourne, take the Eastern Freeway and EastLink toll road and exit onto the Maroondah Highway. Continue on the highway through Ringwood and Lilydale until you reach Coldstream. Here, take the left-hand exit to the Melba Highway – Yering Station is 8km (5 miles) away, on the right-hand side of the road. Be sure to organise pre-payment of an EastLink trip pass; to do so contact your car-rental company or call 13 54 65. Book ahead to eat at Giant Steps/ Innocent Bystander Winery.

In 1844, surveyor Robert Hoddle followed the course of the Yarra River from Melbourne, travelling through a verdant valley to the east of the town, identify-ing the river's source in a forest on the slopes of Mount Baw Baw and becoming one of the first Europeans to discover this picturesque pocket of Victoria.

When gold was found here in 1851, the indigenous Wurundjeri people were swiftly displaced by miners. In the 1880s, orchards and dairy farms followed, laying the foundations for the notable wineries and cheese producers now based here.

In 2009, bushfires raged through the valley, destroying the towns of Marysville and nearby Kinglake. Renowned vineyards, including Domaine Chandon and Yering Station, lost some vines but retained their buildings.

YERING STATION

The Scottish-born Ryrie brothers discovered the joys of the Yarra Valley even earlier than Robert Hoddle, taking up a grazing licence here in 1838. They kept the Wurundjeri name for their land and planted vine cuttings, resulting in Victoria's first vintage in 1845. Today, **Yering Station** ❶ (38 Melba Highway, Yarra Glen; www.yering.com; Mon–Fri

Enjoying a TarraWarra pinot noir

10am–5pm, Sat–Sun 10am–6pm) continues its winemaking tradition and welcomes visitors to its cellar door, housed in an 1859 building. There's also a magnificently sited wine bar-restaurant-art gallery that sits in attractive landscaped gardens. The property's historic barn hosts the **Yarra Valley Regional Farmers' Market** (www.yarravalleyfood.com.au; third Sun each month, 9am–2pm).

TARRAWARRA MUSEUM OF ART

Leave Yering Station, drive to Yarra Glen and turn right onto the Healesville–Yarra Glen Road. After approximately 10km (6 miles) you'll come to the **TarraWarra Museum of Art ❷** (www.twma.com.au; Tue–Sun 11am–5pm; charge).

Set in an award-winning vineyard, this is one of Australia's most impressive contemporary art galleries, notable for its elegant purpose-designed building by local architect Alan Powell. The curators here draw on the many significant works of Australian contemporary art collected by owners Eva and Marc Besen when putting together the gallery's changing exhibition programme.

There's also a stylish wine bar where you can enjoy tastings of TarraWarra's excellent vintages (try the Chardonnay and Pinot Noir) or sit down for a meal.

HEALESVILLE

Continue along the Healesville–Yarra Glen Road until you reach a fork, then turn right to visit the pretty town of **Healesville ❸**, nestled in the foothills of the Great Dividing Range. Settled during the gold rush, it is now a somewhat sleepy nook that's nudged fully awake only at weekends, when it is inundated with

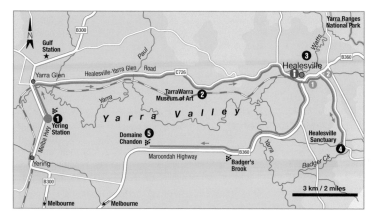

Bottles of red at Giant Steps

day-trippers from Melbourne. The helpful **Yarra Valley Visitor Information Centre** (The Old Courthouse, Harker Street; www.visityarravalley.com.au; daily 9am–5pm) in Healesville can book accommodation, supply free maps and tourist brochures, and recommend activities.

LUNCH OPTIONS

If you're keen to picnic somewhere in the valley, the best place for provisions is **Kitchen & Butcher**, see ①. For a slap-up lunch accompanied by a local tipple, your best option is to head northeast along the Maroondah Highway to the **Giant Steps/Innocent Bystander Winery**, see ②, which has an award-winning pizzeria.

HEALESVILLE SANCTUARY

Home to more than 200 species of Australian birds, mammals and reptiles, **Healesville Sanctuary** ④ (www.zoo.org.au/Healesville; daily 9am–5pm; charge) is a bushland reserve offering close-up encounters with indigenous cuties such as koalas, kangaroos, wombats and emus. To get there, take Badger Creek Road, east out of Healesville town centre.

DOMAINE CHANDON

Continue southeast along the Maroondah Highway to find one of the valley's most spectacularly sited wineries – **Domaine Chandon** ⑤ (Coldstream; www.domainechandon.com.au; daily

10.30am–4.30pm), just a couple of kilometres on from Bella Vedere.

Established by French champagne house Moët & Chandon in 1986 (the valley offers climatically perfect conditions for producing sparkling wines) the winery offers free 30-minute **guided tours** at 11am, 1pm and 3pm daily and a two-hour **wine discovery class** on Sundays, 11am–1pm (bookings essential; charge). End the tour with a glass of bubbly in the winery's spectacular Green Point Brasserie.

Food and drink

① KITCHEN & BUTCHER

258 Maroondah Highway; tel: 5962 2866; www.yarravalleyharvest.com.au; Mon–Fri 10am–6pm, Sat 9am–6pm, Sun 10am–4pm; $

This *providore* stocks a cornucopia of local eatables – many organic and all delectable – plus alluring kitchenware.

② GIANT STEPS/INNOCENT BYSTANDER WINERY

336 Maroondah Highway, Healesville; tel: 5962 6111; www.innocentbystander.com.au; Mon–Fri 10am–10pm, Sat–Sun 8am–10pm; $$

Here at this casual winery, crisp-based pizza hot from the wood oven, with a choice of robust house wine, works supremely well, aided by excellent coffee and perfectly matured cheeses.

Access stunning coastline from the Great Ocean Road

GREAT OCEAN ROAD

Along with Uluru, the Sydney Opera House and the Great Barrier Reef, Victoria's Great Ocean Road is one of Australia's major icons. This route highlights its spectacular scenery and world-famous beach culture.

DISTANCE: 34km (21 miles) from central Melbourne to Werribee Park, plus approximately 270km (167 miles) for this route and 240km (149 miles) back
TIME: Three days
START: Werribee Park
END: Port Campbell National Park
POINTS TO NOTE: It's recommended you rent a car for this excursion. From Melbourne, take the Westgate Freeway (M1) and continue west on the Princes Freeway (M1) before taking the Werribee South/Werribee Park exit and following the signs to Werribee Park Mansion. From Werribee Park, re-join the M1, continue west for 30 minutes to Geelong, then follow signs for the Surfcoast Highway (B100) to the Great Ocean Road. In summer, book accommodation and restaurants well in advance. Bellbrae Harvest Restaurant, Qdos Arts, Chris's Restaurant and the Cape Otway Light Station all offer accommodation.

The Great Ocean Road was built 1919–32 by 3,000 ex-servicemen ('diggers') who had returned to Australia after World War I. It was conceived as a lasting memorial to their many colleagues who lost their lives. Using only picks, shovels and horse-drawn carts, the diggers carved the 243km (151-mile) road out of rock, dense bushland and forest. Today, it's known as one of the world's great coastal drives, and the journey from Torquay to Port Campbell offers spectacular natural scenery, delicious food and wine stops and adrenalin-inducing activities aplenty.

WERRIBEE PARK

Only a 30-minute drive from central Melbourne, **Werribee Park ❶** (K Road, Werribee; www.werribeepark.com.au; Oct–Apr Mon–Fri 10am–6.30pm, Sat–Sun 10am–5pm, other months 10am–4pm; free) is a fascinating first stop.

Werribee Park Mansion
Built for pastoralist Thomas Chirnside, the 60-room **Werribee Park Mansion** dates from 1873–8. It 's the most impressive of the many country resi-

Colourful bollards at Geelong

dences built in the 19th century by the wealthy local landowners and pastoralists known as the 'squattocracy'. An interesting audio tour gives a glimpse of how life was in the mansion's heyday.

A walk around the extensive formal gardens is a highlight, particularly as the estate is the home of the well-respected **Helen Lempriere National Sculpture Award** (www.perpetual.com.au/lempriere) – winning entries from past years are scattered along formal walks, on the sweeping lawns and around the ornamental lake. Between November and April, the bushes in the adjacent **Victoria State Rose Garden** (daily 9am–5.30pm) are in full and fragrant bloom.

In 1923 the property was acquired by the Catholic Church, which used it as a seminary. The Church built several new wings, including one now occupied by the **Mansion Hotel and Spa**. **Joseph's Restaurant**, see ❶, here is an excellent spot for lunch.

Werribee Open Range Zoo

After lunch, consider visiting the **Werribee Open Range Zoo** (www.zoo.org.au; daily 9am–5pm; charge), home to rhinos, giraffes, zebras, hippos, lions, cheetahs and monkeys living in an environment designed to resemble the African savannah.

GEELONG

Continue west along the M1 for 40km (25 miles) to Victoria's second-largest city. **Geelong** ❷ is best known as the gateway to the state's famous Surf Coast, but its long history and picturesque location on Corio Bay make it worth a stop en route. Its name derives from Jillong, the local Wathaurong people's word for 'land' or 'cliffs'. Entering town, follow signs towards the city centre and park in the vicinity of the Geelong Performing Arts Centre.

Geelong Gallery

Geelong Gallery (Little Malop Street; www.geelonggallery.org.au; daily 10am–5pm; guided tours Sat 2pm; free), situated opposite the Performing Arts Centre, has a well-respected permanent collection that includes highlights such as the 1856 painting *View of Geelong* by Eugène von Guérard and Frederick McCubbin's moving 1890 work *A Bush Burial*.

Waterfront

From the gallery, walk north along Gheringhap Street to reach the historic waterfront precinct, which has undergone an extensive refurbishment programme over the past decade.

To the right of Cunningham Pier you'll find the city's popular **Carousel** (1 Eastern Beach Road; Oct–Mar Mon–Fri 10.30am–5pm, Sat until 8pm, Sun until 6pm, Apr–Sept Mon–Fri 11am–4.30pm, Sat 10.30am–6pm, Sun 10.30am–5pm; charge), a steam-driven gem built in New York in 1892 and now housed in a modern glass pavilion.

The Cunningham Pier sign   *Werribee Park Mansion*

Walking to the Eastern Beach Reserve you will pass a troop of colourful **baywalk bollards** painted by local artist Jan Mitchell. At the reserve, an Art Deco **swimming enclosure** (including pavilion and youngsters' pool) takes pride of place.

TORQUAY

Leaving Geelong, take the Surf Coast Highway and drive south for approximately 25 minutes (18km/11 miles) until you arrive at **Torquay** ❸, touted as the 'birthplace of the global surf industry'. Famous for its surf beaches – including the world-renowned breaks Winki Pop and Bells – this rapidly growing town is where global brands such as Rip Curl and Quiksilver originated, and where the **Rip Curl Pro Surf and Music Festival** (www.live.ripcurl.com or www.ripcurl.com.au) is held each Easter. Torquay and Jan Juc beaches offer gentler conditions for novice surfers, and if you're keen to hire a board and wetsuit, or take a surf lesson, check out local companies **Torquay Surfing Academy** (www.torquaysurf.com.au), **Great Ocean Road Surf Tours** (www.gorsurftours.com.au) and **Westcoast Adventure & Surf School** (www.westcoastadventure.org) based in Torquay and Anglesea.

There are safe swimming beaches for families at Cosy Corner and Fisherman's Beach, but remember, many beaches along the Great Ocean Road can be as dangerous as they are beautiful. Rips and undertows abound, and visitors unfamiliar with local conditions should always swim between the red-and-yellow flags at beaches patrolled by trained surf lifesavers. Patrolled beaches include Torquay, Cosy Corner, Jan Juc, Anglesea, Point Roadknight, Fairhaven, Lorne, Wye River, Kennett River, Apollo Bay and Port Campbell. The patrol period runs from late November to mid-April.

Surfworld

Also here is the world's largest surfing museum, **Surfworld** (Surf City Plaza, Beach Road; www.surfworld.com.au; daily 9am–5pm; charge). Full of surfing artefacts and memorabilia, the museum is home to the Australian Surfing Hall of Fame and a cinema screening surfing films. The **Torquay Visitor Information Centre** (http://visitgreatoceanroad.org.au; daily 9am–5pm) is next door.

ANGLESEA TO FAIRHAVEN

The Great Ocean Road officially starts at Torquay. Follow the highway signs to Anglesea, a 20-minute drive through bushland. For a memorable meal en route, turn off the Great Ocean Road at Gundrys Road, take the first right and then the first left to reach **Bellbrae Harvest Restaurant**, see ❷.

Anglesea

Known for its wide front beach, sheer cliffs and coastal heathland, **Anglesea**

Decorated boards at Surfworld

④ is surrounded by national parkland and is a hive of activity during summer, when thousands of families from Melbourne pack their boogie boards and bathers and make the pilgrimage for their annual beach holiday.

Respected local outfit **Eco-Logic Environmental Services** (3 Camp Road; www.ecologic.net.au; charge) offers activities including snorkel tours, guided walks and rockpool rambles. If you play a round at the 18-hole **Anglesea Golf Club** (45 Golf Links Road; www.angleseagolfclub.com.au; daily 11am–sunset; charge), look out for the many kangaroos grazing nonchalantly on the course.

Aireys Inlet

From Anglesea, the road hugs the coastline and offers spectacular views. The next town is sleepy **Aireys Inlet ⑤**, home to the landmark **Split Point Lighthouse** and excellent **A La Grècque** restaurant, café and bar, see **③**. An easy and clearly signed 3.5km (2-mile) clifftop walk starts near the lighthouse and offers wonderful coastal views.

Fairhaven

Adjacent to Aireys Inlet is the exclusive hamlet of **Fairhaven ⑥**, where huge, privately owned beach properties are scattered throughout native bushland. The surf beach here is one of the most beautiful – and unpredictable – in Victoria. Only swim if lifesavers are on duty. From Fairhaven, it's a winding 20-minute drive to the next stop, Lorne.

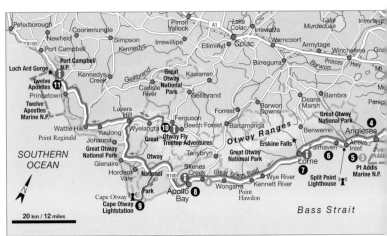

Surfing at Torquay

LORNE

Set between the sparkling waters of Loutit Bay and the forests of the Otway Ranges, **Lorne** ❼ is the most popular holiday destination on the Great Ocean Road and it's packed with facilities – and, often, people. The beach is perfect for families, with gentle waves lapping a wide stretch of golden sand, and the main street is crammed with cafés, shops and a cinema.

In summer Lorne plays host to two popular events. During the New Year holiday period, the Falls Music and Arts Festival (www.fallsfestival.com), one of Australia's most popular live-music events, is held near Erskine Falls. A week or so later, the famous Pier to Pub open water swim (www.lornesurfclub. com.au) attracts 4,000 swimmers from around Australia and overseas.

Qdos Arts

To escape the mayhem, enjoy breakfast, coffee or lunch at **Qdos Arts** (35 Allenvale Road; www.qdosarts.com; Thur–Mon 9am–5.30pm, Tue and Wed holiday periods only), an attractive complex set in tranquil bushland on the hill behind town, with an art gallery, pottery studio, treehouse accommodation and café-restaurant.

To get there, turn left at the roundabout next to the **Lorne Visitor Information Centre** (15 Mountjoy Parade; http://visitgreatoceanroad.org.au; daily 9am–5pm) and drive up Otway Street until you reach a roundabout at the top of the hill. Allenvale Road is the second exit from the roundabout.

Erskine Falls

From Lorne, you can enjoy bushwalks in the nearby national park. The most popular of these is to dramatic **Erskine Falls**, a series of waterfalls cascading into a beautiful gully filled with native tree ferns. To access the falls, drive up Otway Street, turn right at William Street and continue into Erskine Falls Road. The falls are a 20-minute hike down a steep staircase.

LORNE TO APOLLO BAY

Leaving Lorne you'll enter the Great Ocean Road's most stunning section,

with sheer cliffs and majestic ocean views on one side and the Great Otway National Park on the other. After passing through the holiday hamlets of Wye River and Kennett River, you'll reach Skenes Creek and the neighbouring town of Apollo Bay after an hour's drive. This winding and dangerous stretch of road is exhausting to drive, so when you reach **Skenes Creek**, consider resting over a meal at the magnificently located **Chris's Restaurant**, see ➍, which offers panoramic views of the coastline. **Apollo Bay** ➑ is a popular, unpretentious resort with great beaches.

GREAT OTWAY NATIONAL PARK

The **Great Otway National Park** covers 103,000 hectares (255,000 acres) of ancient rainforest, heathlands and woodlands. The most spectacular stretch of the park begins approximately 6km (3.75 miles) west of Apollo Bay. Popular walking tracks include Triplet Falls, Stevenson's Falls, Little Aire, Distillery Creek Circuit and the multiday epic **Great Ocean Walk** (www.greatoceanwalk.info). For details, contact the **Parks Victoria Information Centre** (www.parkweb.vic.gov.au) or the **Great Ocean Road Visitor Centre** at Apollo Bay (100 Great Ocean Road; http://visitgreatoceanroad.org.au; daily 9am–5pm).

Cape Otway Lightstation
The **Cape Otway Lightstation** ➒ (Great Ocean Road, Cape Otway; www.lightstation.com; daily 9am–5pm; charge) is a 30-minute drive from Apollo Bay, veering left off the Great Ocean Road after 18.5km (11.5 miles) onto the Otway Lighthouse Road. Constructed in 1848, this is the oldest surviving lighthouse in Australia. The station runs daily off-road **Lightkeeper's Shipwreck Discovery tours** (10am–noon and 2–4pm) and offers accommodation in its historic lighthouse keepers' cottages. From May to October, it's a popular spot for whale spotting.

Otway Fly Treetop Walk
Approximately 54km/36 miles from Apollo Bay is the spectacular **Otway Fly Treetop Adventures** ➓ (www.otwayfly.com; daily 9am–5pm; charge), a 600-metre (2,000ft) steel walkway perched 25 metres (80ft) up in the rainforest treetops, providing a walk within a canopy of myrtle beech, blackwood and mountain ash. To get there, turn onto the Colac Road from Lavers Hill and follow the road signs.

PORT CAMPBELL NATIONAL PARK

No photo can do true justice to the utterly magnificent **Port Campbell National Park** (www.parkweb.vic.gov.au). This stretch of coastline from Princetown to Peterborough is best-known for the world-famous **Twelve Apostles** ⓫, giant rockstacks left isolated from the mainland by the erosive power of the ocean. A visitor centre at the Twelve Apostles

A pair of Apostles

tells you about the geology and history of the area, and a tunnel under the Great Ocean Road leads to the viewing platforms. The rest of the coastline is home to blowholes, gorges, sea canyons and majestic cliffs.

Loch Ard Gorge

This gorge, 5.5km (3.5 miles) east of Port Campbell, witnessed a tragic shipwreck in 1878. Information panels tell the gripping tale of the clipper *Loch Ard*, the 52 passengers who drowned when it was wrecked on the reef, and the two young people who survived.

From Port Campbell, the fastest return route to Melbourne is via the inland town of Colac. The trip will take about three hours.

Food and drink

① JOSEPH'S RESTAURANT

Mansion Hotel and Spa, Werribee Park, K Road, Werribee; tel: 9731 4000; www.lancemore.com.au; daily 6.30–10.30am, noon–2.30pm and 6.30–10.30pm; $$$
Settings don't come much better than this, and fortunately the menu and wine list at this hotel restaurant live up to the surroundings. The set lunch menus are extraordinarily good value, and afternoon tea is served daily in the foyer between 3–5pm.

② BELLBRAE HARVEST RESTAURANT

45 Portreath Road, Bellbrae; tel: 5266 2100; http://bellbraeharvestrestaurant.com.au; Fri noon–3pm, Fri–Sat dinner from 5pm, Sat–Sun 9.30–11.30am, noon–3pm; $$
In summer outdoor tables overlook a picturesque dam; in winter meals are served in front of an open fire. Bellbrae's innovative menu travels the globe, and does so utilising the very best of local ingredients along the way.

③ A LA GRÈCQUE

60 Great Ocean Road, Aireys Inlet; www.alagrecque.com.au; tel: 5289 6922; Dec–Mar daily 9am–11.30am, 12.30–2.30pm, 6–10pm (off season Apr–Nov Wed–Sun, closed mid-June–mid-Aug; $$
There are no views on offer at this hugely popular taverna, just stylish surroundings and an unpretentious and delicious Greek and Mediterranean-flavoured menu. Owners Pam and Kosta Talimanidis have been operating restaurants along the coast for decades. It's also a popular coffee stop.

④ CHRIS'S RESTAURANT

280 Skenes Creek Road, Apollo Bay; tel: 5237 6411; www.chriss.com.au; daily 8.30–10am, noon–2pm and 6–10pm; $$$$
Perched high in the Otways overlooking Bass Strait, Chris's is known throughout Australia for its spectacular setting and fresh seafood dishes, which are cooked simply but with great expertise. It is worth booking one of the villas to stay here overnight so that you can admire the sunset over dinner.

DIRECTORY

Hand-picked hotels and restaurants to suit all budgets and tastes, organised by area, plus select nightlife listings, an alphabetical listing of practical information and an overview of the best books and films to give you a flavour of the city.

Hilton Melbourne South Wharf's lobby

ACCOMMODATION

Melbourne offers the full gamut of accommodation types, but is particularly blessed when it comes to apartment and boutique hotels. The best location for visitors is the city centre and immediate surrounds, although St Kilda and South Yarra both have their allure – St Kilda is especially beloved by backpackers and South Yarra is the location of choice for visiting celebs. In the CBD, the best hotels tend to be located on or around Collins, Little Collins and Queen streets, but there are also attractive options scattered across the grid and on the East Melbourne, Fitzroy and Carlton fringes.

Last-minute accommodation is usually available, the only exception being when high-profile sporting festivals and events, such as the Australian Open (January), Australian Grand Prix (March), AFL Grand Final (September) and Spring Racing Carnival (November), are being held; at these times room rates rise and available rooms can be scarce, meaning that you should book well in advance.

Price for a double room for one night without breakfast:
$$$$ = over A$220
$$$ = A$150–220
$$ = A$80–150
$ = below A$80

Central Melbourne

The Adelphi
187 Flinders Lane; tel: 8080 8888; www.adelphi.com.au; $$$–$$$$
When it opened in 1990, this boutique hotel was as glam as they come. A showcase of the trademark visual style of local architectural doyens Denton Corker Marshall (who designed the Melbourne Museum), it's particularly notable for a whimsical rooftop lap pool, which extends out over the street and has a glass bottom – not recommended for swimmers who are afraid of heights! Although the interior is looking a bit on the dated side these days, the rooftop bar and basement restaurant (see page 110) retain their hip credentials.

Alto Hotel on Bourke Street
636 Bourke Street; tel: 8608 5500; www.altohotel.com.au; $$$–$$$$
Close to Southern Cross Railway Station and the Docklands, Alto Hotel markets itself as being environmentally friendly. Its emissions are offset, 'green-choice' electricity is used, rainwater is utilised for cleaning, plastics are kept to a minimum and waste is recycled. Rooms and apartments have a warm colour scheme and bathrooms have granite features; apartments have a kitchenette. The cosy lounge, bar-restaurant and relaxation room give the place an edge.

The Adelphi   *Room with a view*

Hotel Causeway

275 Little Collins Street; tel: 03-9660 8888; www.hotelcauseway.com.au; $$$–$$$$

A simple but stylish option, smack-bang in the centre of town, Hotel Causeway sports neat and nifty rooms. There's a gym and steam room, and a small roof terrace. The rack rate is perhaps overpriced, but the weekend and summer specials are worth checking out.

Citadines on Bourke

131-135 Bourke Street; tel: 9039 8888; www.citadines.com; $$$

Blessed with a tip-top location in the middle of town, there's a bewildering selection of great restaurants, bars and theatres to choose from right outside the door of this place. The rooms here are spacious and clean. Wi-fi is fast and free, but if you arrive by car you're going to have to fork out a pricey $A30 to park beneath the hotel. There's a small gym and pool – ask for a room on the upper floors for killer views over the city.

City Centre Hotel

22 Little Collins Street; tel: 9654 5401; www.citycentrebudgethotel.com.au; $–$$

This family run backpacker joint is in the midst of one of the most happening bar enclaves in the city, close to Parliament Station and the Treasury Gardens. There's free WiFi and internet, a roof terrace and laundry facilities. Rooms have a television, fridge, fans (no air-conditioning) and tea-and-coffee-making facilities; bathrooms are shared.

Crown Metropol

8 Whiteman Street, Southbank; tel: 9292 8888; www.crownmetropol.com.au; $$$$

If a contemporary luxury hotel is what you're looking for, this is where you should be staying. Pamper yourself in the exclusive day spa, Isika, catch the breathtaking city views from 28, the sky bar on that level or take the plunge in one of the infinity pools.

Greenhouse Backpackers Melbourne

228 Flinders Lane; tel: 1800-249 207; www.friendlygroup.com.au; $

The institutional atmosphere won't be for everyone, but this clean, no-nonsense backpacker joint near Flinders Street Railway Station offers the cheapest singles accommodation in the central city (couples might want to shop around for a cheaper alternative). There's key-card access for every room and the hostel is next to a 24-hour police station, so it is as safe and secure as they come. It also offers free internet access and a self-catering kitchen.

Hilton Melbourne South Wharf

2 Convention Centre Place, South Wharf; tel: 9027 2000; www.hiltonmelbourne.com.au; $$$$

This hotel's 396 rooms feature floor-to-ceiling windows with views of the city and the Yarra River, and for some great dining and drinking options, all you have to do is go downstairs, where two classy venues are located. Stylish Sotano Wine + Tapas

Clean lines at Jasper Hotel

(www.sotano.com.au) was awarded Bar of the Year at the AHA Awards (2010), while Nuevo37 (www.nuevo37.com.au) serves Spanish-inspired Australian fare.

Hotel Lindrum

26 Flinders Street; tel: 9668 1111; www.hotellindrum.com.au; $$$$

Once home to a well-known billiard hall, this attractive building is now one of the city's best boutique hotels. Close to Federation Square, it is within easy access of both CBD amenities and the sporting precinct along the Yarra. The hotel's 59 rooms and suites are as stylish as they are spacious; the deluxe versions also offer great views. There's a sleek restaurant and bar on the ground floor where you can relax after a day's exploration.

Hotel Windsor

111 Spring Street; tel: 9633 6000; www.thewindsor.com.au; $$$$

Gentility is the word that springs to mind when this grande dame of the city's hostelries is mentioned, and although the possibility of a hip renovation has been much discussed, traditional decor and service currently reign supreme. Located opposite Parliament House, the hotel's rooms and public spaces are conservatively decorated and will please most guests. The traditional afternoon tea served daily in the lounge is a Melbourne institution.

Jasper Hotel

489 Elizabeth Street; tel: 8327 2777; www.jasperhotel.com.au; $$–$$$

Once the worthy but drab YWCA, the Jasper opened in 2007 after a huge renovation and now sports a rich colour scheme and funky aesthetic, making its claim to the boutique tag credible (if not compelling). Another renovation, completed in late 2014, has given it a really contemporary feel. The hotel's location next to popular Queen Victoria Market means it is vibrant during the day but quiet at night.

The Langham Melbourne

One Southgate Avenue, Southbank; tel: 8696 8888; http://melbourne.langham hotels.com.au; $$$$

One of the most lauded luxury hotels in Melbourne, the Langham has innovative facilities such as 'Service Stylists', paying attention to every detail. Having been around since 1865, the brand is also known for its excellence. The hotel overlooks the Yarra River and is surrounded by countless dining and shopping options.

Mercure Welcome Melbourne

265 Little Bourke Street; tel: 9639 0555; www.accorhotels.com.au/hotel/mercure-welcome-melbourne; $$–$$$

No boutique or luxury credentials here, just clean, neat and well-equipped rooms in a central location. The major department stores are around the corner, and the city's major tram route is directly in front of the hotel, making trips around Melbourne easy as pie. Check for online specials – they can be half the rack rate.

The Langham jacuzzi　　　　　　　　　　　　*The exterior of the Langham*

Oaks On William

350 William Street; tel: 8329 6600; www.oaks
hotelsresorts.com/oaks-on-william; $$$

One of Melbourne's newest hotels, Oaks On William occupies a prime spot opposite Flagstaff Gardens, on the fringe of the city and overlooking the CBD and central entertainment strips that are so easy to access from it doors. Unusually, many rooms come equipped with a kitchen and, since you're nice and close to the brilliant Queen Vic Market, you can cook up a storm and fully enjoy the fresh fruits of this great city. On the downside, WiFi is not included.

Ovolo Laneways

19 Little Bourke Street; tel: 8692 0777;
www.ovolohotels.com; $$$

A very funky boutique crash pad in the midst of the laneways that act as the arteries to Melbourne's pumping hipster heart. Reflecting their surroundings, the rooms here are low-lit, uber trendy and, often, somewhat resonant with the activity of the city (if this is likely to bother you, request a room that doesn't look out on Little Bourke Street or the lane). A variety of cool rooms are available, all with Wi-fi, ranging from studios (complete with beanbag chairs) to suites, some with kitchenettes, desks and separate living and sleeping areas. The Penthouse suite is fantastic. Breakfast to go is available in the lobby.

Park Hyatt

1 Parliament Square, offParliament Place; tel: 9224 1234; www.melbourne.park.hyatt.
com; $$$$

The central yet secluded location of this luxury pile opposite St Patrick's Cathedral almost seems at odds with its ostentatious decor, which looks towards Las Vegas for inspiration. All is forgiven, though, when the spacious rooms with their king-sized beds and Italian marble baths are inspected. Facilities – including a well-equipped gym, indoor swimming pool, spa and excellent restaurant – are among the best in town.

Punt Hill Little Bourke

11–17 Cohen Place; tel: 9916 8888;
www.punthill.com.au; $$$

This attractive modern building in Melbourne's Chinatown offers comfortable apartments with kitchenettes and laundry facilities, while public facilities include a gym and an indoor lap pool. As befits the location, the building has been designed to meet feng shui requirements and there's a ground-floor Chinese restaurant. Melbourne's major theatres are only a curtain call away.

Robinsons in the City

405 Spencer Street; tel: 9329 2552;
www.robinsonsinthecity.com.au; $$$

Housed in an 1850s building that was Melbourne's first commercial bakery, this B&B on the edge of the city centre offers an intimate accommodation experience. Of the six rooms on offer, five have private bathrooms opposite the bedroom and one has an attached en-suite; all have

free WiFi and air-conditioning. Breakfast is prepared by the owner and served in the old bakehouse. The location can be a little bit off-putting at night.

The Sebel Melbourne, Flinders Lane

321 Flinders Lane; tel: 96294088; www.thesebel.com; $$$$

Super central, offering mega spacious apartments suitable for swinging cats or whatever else takes your fancy. Fine for families, couples and business people who like plenty of room to stretch out in self-contained private accommodation, as well as the ability to self cater. No need for a car – everything is walkable from right outside the door. Don't expect fresh towels every day, however – while the apartments are service several times weekly, this isn't a standard hotel.

Treasury On Collins

394 Collins Street; tel: 8535 8535; www.treasuryoncollins.com.au; $$$$

This entire building was, briefly, converted into a popular apartment hotel, but in 2013 the owners reclaimed them. Well, most of them did – you can still rent a number of one- and two-bedroom luxury suites, including a loft apartment, in this cracking central location, all with access to a fitness room / gym and high-speed internet. The apartments' close proximity to Café Vue (see page 33), which serves one of the best breakfasts in the city, is just one reason to love these apartments.

Tune Hotel

609 Swanston Street; 9347 3027; www.tunehotels.com; $$

Undoubtedly one of the best budget options in Melbourne, where you pay for your room, and then fork out for other services – such as wifi and housekeeping –according to your needs, so you don't end up paying for anything that you don't want or use. It's a clean place, with no-frills rooms that you wont be swinging any cats in, but are perfectly adequate for sleeping. Doubles, twins and family rooms are available, alone with accessible rooms, and there's parking available underneath for A$15

Sofitel Melbourne on Collins

25 Collins Street; tel: 9653 0000; www.sofitelmelbourne.com.au; $$$$

Located in the 'Paris End' of Collins Street, the Sofitel has rooms starting on level 36 of a high-rise tower. All rooms have spectacular views; if your budget allows, opt for a luxury room or a suite, as the standard room is slightly cramped. There are bars and restaurants galore, a business centre and a fitness centre.

Stamford Plaza

111 Little Collins Street; tel: 9659 1000; www.stamford.com.au/spm; $$$$

Located at the top end of town, the Stamford Plaza has amenities aplenty, including an indoor/outdoor pool, a restaurant, a bar and two gyms. All suites feature kitchenettes and bath-spas. The somewhat fussy decor here won't

please fans of the minimalist aesthetic, but services such as complimentary overnight shoeshining may compensate.

Vibe Savoy

630 Little Collins Street; tel: 03-9622 8888; www.vibehotels.com.au; $$$

This intimate hotel within a 1920s heritage building promotes an elegant, club-like atmosphere. The fresh and hip vibe appeals to younger travellers, with the hotel in the midst of the bustle of the city. At the end of the day, slink into the trendy Alexander Bar for a refreshing cocktail.

The Victoria Hotel

215 Little Collins Street; tel: 03-9669 0000; www.victoriahotel.com.au; $$

A basic, but very practical accommodation option for those who want to be central but not pay through the nose for a room they're only going to sleep in. Bargain-lovers will be thrilled by this place, as prices are super-cheap. There's a rooftop gym, pool, sauna and spa, as well as an internet café, bar and restaurant.

Westin Melbourne

205 Collins Street; tel: 9635 2222; www.westinmelbourne.com; $$$$

The Westin has an outstanding location overlooking the City Square, St Paul's Cathedral and leafy Collins Street. Decor is stylishly understated, featuring muted colour schemes and excellent Australian contemporary art. The wellness centre features a lap pool, spa, gym and steam room. Top marks go to the bar and restaurant spaces that allow you to relax indoors or on a terrace overlooking the City Square.

Docklands

Docklands Apartments – Grand Mercure

23 St Mangos Lane; tel: 03-9641 7503; www.docklandsservicedapartments.com. au; $$$$

This Grand Mercure setting is the largest serviced apartment complex by the waterfront in Melbourne. Next to the vibrant Waterfront City and close to the shopping district, it caters to both business and leisure travellers. The rooms are sleek and comfortable, matching its waterfront setting.

The Sebel Melbourne, Docklands

Corner Aquitania Way & Marmion Place, New Quay; tel: 9641 7503; www.thesebel. com; $$$

Similar set up to the apartments under the same name on Flinders Street: here you will find generously proportioned one-, two- and three-bedroom apartments and studios, situated in the ultra-modern Docklands district on the waterfront. The self-contained rooms are every bit as swanky as the city venue, but the surrounding area is decidedly less vibrant. However, it's very handy for sporting events at the nearby Etihad/Docklands Stadium.

A funky room at the Sebel, Melbourne

Carlton and Parkville

Downtowner on Lygon

66 Lygon Street; tel: 9663 5555;
www.downtowner.com.au; $$$

The location here is perfect – halfway between the city centre and the bohemian enclave of Carlton. Rooms are attractive and well equipped, with king-sized beds and small en-suites. Guests have free access to the Melbourne City Baths' pool and gym nearby. There's a restaurant and bar, but the Lygon Street alternatives are more alluring.

Fitzroy

Brooklyn Arts Hotel

48-50 George Street; tel: 9419 9328;
www.brooklynartshotel.com.au; $$$

A unique boutique option nestled in the arms of George Street in the heart of Fitzroy, with bags of character and charm. This is a great option for people who like their accommodation to come complete with personality (found in both the building and the proprietor Maggie) and memorable décor. From here it's very easy to reach and explore arty and fashionable Gertrude Street, or to enjoy the bars and restaurants found along Brunswick Street and Smith Street.

The Nunnery

116 Nicholson Street; tel: 9419 8637;
www.nunnery.com.au; $–$$

This place offers three tiers of accommodation and is deservedly popular. Housed in three historic buildings, its city-edge location faces the Carlton Gardens. The hostel occupies a former nunnery and offers a choice of budget single, double and dorm rooms, while the guesthouse has comfortable single, double and family rooms. At the top tier is the townhouse, with stylishly renovated singles and doubles. Bathrooms are shared, there are fans and heaters in all rooms and there's a communal kitchen and lounge in each building.

East Melbourne

Knightsbridge Apartments

101 George Street; tel: 9470 9100;
www.knightsbridgeapartments.com.au;
$$–$$$

In an excellent location close to Fitzroy Gardens, Melbourne Cricket Ground and the busy shopping and entertainment precinct of Bridge Road in Richmond, these serviced studio apartments offer WiFi, an en-suite bathroom, a kitchenette with basic equipment and air-conditioning. The decor is pleasant and rates are reasonable, particularly the last-minute deals.

Prahran, South Yarra and Toorak

The Como Melbourne – MGallery Collection

630 Chapel Street, South Yarra; tel: 9825 2222; www.accorhotels.com/gb/hotel-8801-the-como-melbourne-mgallery-collection; $$$$

Many of the rich and famous wouldn't stay anywhere else. The Como offers suites with king-sized beds, spacious

en-suites and sitting areas; some have private Japanese gardens while others have spas, balconies and study areas. There's an indoor/outdoor swimming pool, as well as a spa, sauna, gym and sundeck. Rates are extremely reasonable considering the level of service on offer, and the hotel's location is close to the shopping and eating temptations of Chapel Street and Toorak Road.

The Cullen

164 Commercial Road, Prahran; tel: 9098 1555; www.artserieshotels.com.au/cullen; $$$

Launched in 2009, the enigmatic Art Series Group of hotels (of which there are six in total, three in Melbourne – see the Olsen and the Blackman, below) are all inspired by and dedicated to an Australian artist of note – this one revolved around the work of Adam Cullen – and original work by this artist is on display around the venue. Rooms include comfortable and cool Art Series signature beds and have kitchenette facilities, so you can explore the fresh produce available at nearby Prahran Market and make a snack or light meal while looking out over this trendy end of town. There's also a gym, underground parking and a choice of places to eat. Pay extra for bed and breakfast. Keep your eye out for discounted rates during sales.

The Hatton Hotel

65 Park Street, South Yarra; tel: 9868 4800;

www.hatton.com.au; $$$

Brilliantly positioned close to the Botanical Gardens, this is an affordable boutique option for those who want to stay on the periphery of the city centre without having all the bustle right outside the window. There are various rooms styles available, with the ones at the back being preferable if you do like things very quiet – but the convenience of having a tram stop outside the door is worth the odd rattling sound, even if you're at the front. Head up to the rooftop terrace for a cracking view of Melbourne's skyline. Breakfast is continental (but generous) and Wi-fi is free and available in the rooms.

The Lyall

14 Murphy Street, South Yarra; tel: 9868 8222; www.thelyall.com; $$$$

This boutique hotel located on a leafy residential street off the upmarket South Yarra shopping and eating strip has the feel and decor of a private club. The suites feature elegant decor with plenty of luxurious touches – you are bound to sleep well here. The in-house spa, posh restaurant and glam champagne bar ensure a sybaritic stay.

The Olsen

637-641 Chapel Street, South Yarra; tel: 9040 1222; www.artserieshotels.com.au/ olsen; $$$

Another innovative property run by the impressive Art Series Hotels

mob, this one is inspired by and features some of the original work of the Australian landscape artist Dr John Olsen. Centrally situated on Chapel Street, near public transport into the city, there are 229 five-star suites here, plus a day spa and two cracking restaurants.

Albert Park

The Blackman

452 St Kilda Road; tel: 9039 1444; www.artserieshotels.com.au/blackman; $$$

The Art Series Group of hotels are all inspired by and dedicated to a noted Australian artist. The buildings feature original work by said artist – in this case Charles Blackman – which here adds a lovely warm touch to a place that can appear quite clinical from the outside. There are 209 spacious suites here, boasting balconies overlooking Albert Park. Enjoy easy access to the city and St Kilda from here.

Hotel Charsfield

478 St Kilda Road; tel: 9866 5511; www.charsfield.com; $$$

Housed in a period building, this hotel places greater import on character over ostentatious class, but still delivers fantastic customer service. Very centrally located for the city and Melbourne's more interesting suburbs. Trams run right past. Boasting modern and very clean rooms in a heritage setting, the generous bed-and-breakfast deal is the way to go.

Royce Hotel

379 St Kilda Road, tel: 9677 9900; www.roycehotels.com.au; $$$$

Centrally located between a triumvirate of attractions, the Royce looks out over Albert Park and the Botanic Gardens, and is within easy striking distance of both Melbourne city and the funky eating, drinking and shopping suburbs of St Kilda, Toorak Road and Chapel Street. There are 100 modern rooms available at this five-star boutique hotel on the city's premier boulevard, but they're in hot demand during Melbourne's many sporting events and festivals.

St Kilda

Base Backpackers Melbourne

17 Carlisle Street, St Kilda; tel: 8598 6200; www.stayatbase.com/hostels/australia-hostels/base-backpackers-melbourne; $

This sleek operation markets itself as Australia's hippest hostel. Four- to eight-bed dorms have bunk beds, air-conditioning, security lockers and private en-suites; the 'Sanctuary Floor' is for females only. There are laundry facilities and an internet café, and St Kilda's lively café, bar and beach scene is right on the doorstep.

Novotel Melbourne St Kilda

16 The Esplanade; tel: 9525 5522; www.novotelstkilda.com.au; $$$–$$$$

Occupying a fantastic location in Melbourne's funkiest beachside suburb. There's a bar and grill on site, but why

eat in when you're so close to St Kilda's bars and restaurants? Comes with a buffet breakfast. The 211 rooms are less than palatial, but the comfy beds make up for that. There's a heated pool if a dip in the Bay doesn't appeal, plus a fitness centre and 24-hour room service. No thrills, but if you score a special it's not bad for the price.

The Prince

2 Acland Street, St Kilda;
tel: 9536 1111; www.theprince.com.au;
$$$–$$$$
The über-stylish Prince was designed by the edgy architectural firm Wood Marsh and has worn well in the decade since it opened. Rooms feature deluxe linen, distinctive artwork and soothing colour schemes; the suites have fabulous views of Port Phillip Bay. The hotel's Aurora Spa is probably the best one in Melbourne, and the same encomium applies to the in-house Circa Restaurant.

Yarra Valley and Healesville

Balgownie Estate Vineyard Resort & Spa

Corner of Melba Highway and Gulf Road, Yarra Glen; tel: 9730 0700;
www.balgownieestate.com.au; $$$$
This resort and spa has elegant spa suites with views of the landscaped gardens and rolling vineyards. After wining and dining, make a booking at the Natskin Spa Retreat to de-stress for a few hours.

Healesville Sanctuary Park Cottages

85 Badger Avenue; tel: 03-5962 2904;
www.sanctuarypark.com.au; $$$
Only an hour's drive from Melbourne, Sanctuary Park is the perfect country escape. The private cottage accommodations offer amazing views of the surrounding mountains, wineries and vast landscape, and – of course – the wildlife sanctuary (see page 90) is close by.

Great Ocean Road

Cumberland Lorne Resort

150 Mountjoy Parade, Lorne; tel: 03-5289 4444; www.cumberland.com.au; $$$
The Cumberland offers suites with wonderful views and complimentary recreational activities, right in the heart of this friendly town. The contemporary open-plan living in each apartment gives ample of space to unwind; with full kitchen and laundry amenities and a corner spa bath.

Seaview Motel and Apartments

6 Thomson Street, Apollo Bay; tel: 5237 6660; www.seaviewmotel.com.au; $$
A family-run business, Seaview is located in the popular holiday town of Apollo Bay, along the Great Ocean Road and Otway Ranges, within easy reach of the fabulous sea and world-class beaches that line this curvaceous coast. The rooms are clean and modern with free WiFi, and there is also a common barbecue area for mingling with other guests and sharing tips and stories.

At work in a restaurant kitchen

RESTAURANTS

Melbourne has one of the most impressive and diverse food scenes in the world – you will find outlets here serving cuisines from all around the planet, with myriad options to suit every tastebud and budget. Most places are found in the city centre or inner suburbs, with hot spots being Fitzroy, St Kilda and East Brunswick (north of Carlton). The restaurants listed below are all extremely popular, so making a booking is highly recommended.

Central Melbourne

Becco

11–25 Crossley Street; tel: 9663 3000; www.becco.com.au; Mon–Sat noon–3pm and 6–11pm; $$$
This buzzy and stylish Italian restaurant-bar is tucked down a laneway at the eastern end of Bourke Street. It's hugely popular with city residents, who come to enjoy the home-style Italian cooking, including pasta classics and comfort mains such as *cotoletta* (crumbed veal cutlet). The bar serves

> Price guide for a two-course dinner for one with a glass of house wine:
> $$$$ = over A$80
> $$$ = A$60–80
> $$ = A$45–60
> $ = below A$45

inexpensive lunches during the day and tasty bar snacks at night.

Cookie

Level 1, Curtain House, 252 Swanston Street; tel: 9663 7660; www.cookie.net.au; daily noon–11pm (bar noon–3am); $
Boho Melbourne loves to drink at this excellent bar, and those in the know also eat their fill at Cookie's funky restaurant, where the inventive and tasty Thai cuisine pleases both palate and wallet. Don't expect a quiet or leisurely meal – this joint jumps, and staff will encourage you to kick on to the bar rather than linger at your table.

Ezard

187 Flinders Lane: tel: 9639 6811; www.ezard.com.au; Mon–Fri noon–2.30pm and 6–10.30pm, Sat 6–10.30pm; $$$$
The sophisticated decor of this restaurant in the basement of the Adelphi hotel (see page 100) is more than matched by the menu, which features stunningly presented dishes conceived with confidence and executed with a great deal of skill. Owner/chef Teage Ezard uses the finest local produce, and has a particular love of Chinese and Thai fusion styles, although he also flirts with Middle Eastern flavours.

Gingerboy

27–29 Crossley Street; tel: 9662 4200;

www.gingerboy.com.au; Mon–Fri noon–2.30pm, Mon–Sat 6pm–late; $$

Southeast Asian hawker food gets a designer makeover here, complete with excellent cocktails and a wine list of Old and New World labels that harmonise well with the abundant hot, spicy, fishy and tangy flavours. The most notable of a spate of new and innovative Asian eateries in town.

Il Bàcaro

168 Little Collins Street; tel: 9654 6778; www.ilbacaro.com.au; Mon–Sat noon–3pm and 6–10.30pm; $$$

With its sleek and sexy Italian decor, flirtatious Italian staff and skilfully cooked modern versions of classic Italian dishes, il Bàcaro has remained a perennial favourite on the Melbourne dining scene. The menu rarely surprises (neither does it disappoint), and the bar is a great spot for an *aperitivo*.

The Little Mule Company

19 Somerset Place; tel: 9670 4904; www.thelittlemule.com; Mon–Fri 7.30am–3.30pm, Sat 9.30am–3.30pm; $

That essential one-stop-shop for all the times when you wake up with a desperate craving for great coffee, baked eggs on avocado toast, and a new single-speed bicycle. Phew. Hiding away down an alleyway in central Melbourne, this little cafe is part altar to the awesomeness of bikes, and part chapel for the celebration of good coffee. The breakfast/brunch/lunch menu is good too, though, and your juice will be served in a jam jar.

Longrain

44 Little Bourke Street; tel: 9671 3151; www.longrain.com.au; Fri noon–3pm, Mon–Fri 6–11pm, Sat 5.30–11pm, Sun 5.30–10pm; $$$

An outpost of the famous Sydney establishment, Longrain is known for its modern Thai-inspired cuisine. In a huge warehouse-style space in Chinatown, the restaurant's long and round communal tables are inevitably full of glamorous young things sharing a spicy meal together.

Merchant

Rialto 495 Collins Street; tel: 9614 7688; www.merchantov.com; Mon–Fri 7am–11pm, Sat noon–11pm; $$$

Chef Guy Grossi's latest restaurant, housed in an old red brick building at the Rialto Towers forecourt, is reminiscent of a vibrant and relaxed (but chic) restaurant in Venice. The hearty Northern Italian dishes include a huge range of risottos and polentas alongside grilled fresh seafood and meat. Finish off with gelato or a Venetian trifle.

MoVida

1 Hosier Lane; tel: 9663 3038; www.movida.com.au; daily noon–late; $$–$$$

One of the city's favourite eateries, Movida looks to Madrid for inspiration. Owner/chef Frank Camorra trained in Spain and delivers assured

Seafood pasta at Sarti

tapas and raciones, utilising a mix of top-quality local produce and the best Iberian imports. Dishes range from classic to unexpected, and are consistently delicious. If you have no luck scoring a table, try **Movida Next Door** (Corner Flinders Street and Hosier Lane; Fri noon–midnight, Tue–Thur 5pm–late; $$) or the newer and larger **Movida Aqui** (level 1, 500 Bourke Street; Mon–Fri noon–late, Sat 5pm–late; $$).

Sarti

6 Russell Place; tel: 9639 7822; www.sartirestaurant.com.au; Mon–Fri noon–3pm, Mon–Sat 6pm–late; $$$

The menu here has a classic Italian base but features some intriguing modern twists. The *stuzzichini* (small appetisers designed to be shared) are full of fun and flavour, the *paste* and *risotti* are refined and the mains inevitably incorporate an unusual ingredient or two. Best of all are the desserts, which are worth a visit in their own right.

Supper Inn

15 Celestial Avenue; tel: 9663 4759; daily 5.30pm–2.30am; $

The word 'institution' is often bandied around when talking about the city's eateries, but this is one of the few places that deserve to be described as such. Always crowded (particularly late at night), it has utterly wonderful Cantonese food that puts many of its more expensive neighbours to shame.

Taxi Dining Room

Level 1, Transport Hotel, Federation Square; www.taxikitchen.com.au; tel: 9654 8808; daily noon–3pm and 6–11pm; $$$$

Locals wanting to impress clients or first dates head toward this stylish restaurant in Federation Square – part of the Transport Hotel (www.transporthotel.com.au) complex, overlooking the Yarra – which has one of the most stunning interiors in Melbourne. The impressive modern menu, featuring meals using primarily Asian ingredients, are complemented by an extraordinarily fine wine list.

Vue de Monde

430 Little Collins Street; tel: 9691 3888; www.vuedemonde.com.au; Tue–Fri, Sun noon–2pm, Mon–Sat 6–9.15pm; $$$$

Regularly nominated as one of Australia's two best restaurants, and one of only three venues in Melbourne that can currently boast a three-hat rating (see page 117), Shannon Bennett's Vue de Monde is not for diners after a low-key meal. The chef focuses on produce-driven cuisine using heirloom and organic vegetables and fruits sourced directly from growers and farmers as well as local and sustainable seafood and meat. The space at the top of the Rialto Towers affords a stunning view of the city skyline.

Taxi Dining Room

South Melbourne, Albert Park and St Kilda Road

St Ali
12-18 Yarra Place; tel: 9686 2990; www.stali.com.au; daily 7am–evening; $
You can come to eat in this super cool cafe tucked away in an alley behind Clarendon Street in South Melbourne – and you will be fed well (with the breakfast/brunch/lunch menu including such substantial listings as ham hock cassoulet with black pudding and fried egg) – but in reality, everyone is here for one thing: the coffee. A serious caffeine pusher from the early days, St Ali is one of the institutions that helped put Melbourne in the centre of the coffee-stained world map.

The Olive Tree
19 Park Street, South Melbourne; tel: 9969 9152; www.theolivetree.com.au; Mon–Fri noon–2.30pm, Mon–Sat 6pm–late; $$
Having been in business for almost 45 years, this family run restaurant knows exactly how to please. Famed for steaks and seafood, they also serve a fantastic rack of lamb. Good selection of wines and beers available. Portions are generous, service is fantastic and the ambience is comfortable. Try and get the brilliant bay window.

Hunter's Kitchen & Bar
454 St Kilda Road; tel: 9867 4466; www.hunterskitchen.com.au; Mon–Sat 7am–11pm; $$
From coffee and breakfast through to the after-dinner cheese plate, Hunters provides a warm and welcoming setting to enjoy your eating experience. The menu makes great use of free-range produce, sourced from Victorian providers when possible. Service is extremely friendly and prices are very reasonable. Try the pork belly.

Kamel
19 Victoria Avenue, Albert Park; tel: 9696 1386; www.kamelrestaurant.com; Fri–Sun 8am–3pm and 5pm–10pm, Mon–Sun 5pm–10pm; $
Excellent Moroccan, Turkish and Middle Eastern cuisine served in comfortable and unpretentious surrounds with an authentic North African ambience. Shared plates are the way to go here, so you can try as many of the flavours offered by the menu as possible. Sit inside or in the courtyard in the summer. Takeaway is also available if you want to eat alfresco in one of the many leafy green areas around South Melbourne.

Café Rosco
407D St Kilda Road; tel: 9866 2280; www.caferosco.com.au; Mon–Fri 11.30am–11pm, Sat 5pm–11pm, Sun 5pm–10pm; $
Loved by office workers, tourist and night revellers alike, Café Rosco offers a range of Italian food throughout the day and into the evening - think gourmet pizzas and pastas with fresh home-made sauces, scallopini and

parmas. Quality tucker at fast-food speed – you'll be happily munching within 30 minutes of ordering. Crack into a beer or wine while you dine – they're fully licensed.

Carlton, Parkville and East Brunswick

Abla's

109 Elgin Street, Carlton; tel: 9347 0006; www.ablas.com.au; Thur–Fri noon–3pm, Mon–Sat 6–11pm; $

Abla Amad's delectable home-style Lebanese food has devotees throughout the city. The dated interior perhaps hasn't the style sported by the trendy restaurants of Beirut, but the quality of her cooking could put most of those places to shame. The kibbe and kebabs are delicious, and the spiced pilaf with minced lamb, chicken and almonds is to die for.

Hellenic Republic

434 Lygon Street, East Brunswick; tel: 9381 1222; www.hellenicrepublic.com.au; Sat–Sun 9–11.30am, Fri–Sun noon–4pm, daily 5.30pm–late; $

Melbourne has the largest Greek population of any city outside Greece, so Greek restaurants here can hold their own with any in the old country. This taverna is owned by high-profile chef George Calombaris of Press Club (see page 33) and *MasterChef* fame, and is characterised by a casual atmosphere and a simple menu featuring fish, meat and salads.

Royale Fusion

128-130 Lygon Street, tel: 9639 9383; www.royalefusion.com.au; Sun–Tues and Thurs 5–10.30pm, Fri–Sat 5pm–late; $

When you head out for a bite to eat on Lygon Street, you expect to be savouring Italian herbs rather than Indian spices, but friendly family-run Royal Fusion has been turning heads and teasing tastebuds here since it opened. Authentic flavours, excellent vegetarian and meat options, great service and an interesting Indo-Chinese fusion page in the menu all adds up to a good night of eating. Very reasonably priced too.

Seven Seeds

114 Berkley Street, Carlton; tel: 9347 8664; Mon–Sat 7am–5pm, Sun 8am–5pm; $

A serious front runner in the coolest-coffeehouse-in-town stakes, this bean-roasting joint and caffeine dealership serves a killer cup of the elixir that keeps most of Melbourne operational. Tea, too, is available, from an extensive menu that runs from English breakfast right through to liquorice & lavender. And there is food – damn good food – albeit slightly on the fancy side. Anyone for coffee-roasted carrot salad with fresh ricotta, hazelnuts, pickled onions and a poached egg? Customers' bikes (mostly fixies, naturally) hang from the walls, and public cuppings (coffee tasting) take place here on Wednesdays at 9am and Saturdays at 10am.

Hellenic Republic

Fitzroy

Añada

197 Gertrude Street, Fitzroy; tel: 9415 6101; www.anada.com.au; Mon–Fri 6pm–late, Sat–Sun noon–late; $

This place has an atmosphere and decor that immediately recall Spain, and a menu that could hold its own among the best tapas bars in Andalusia. Choose from an extensive list of simple but memorable tapas and *raciones*, and wash your choice down with a wine or sherry from Spain or Portugal.

Brother Burger and the Marvellous Brew

413, Brunswick Street, tel: 9419 0088; www.brotherburger.com.au; Sun–Thur noon–10pm, Fri–Sat noon–11pm; $

Big burgers. Cold beers. Really, what else do you need? Well, what you get is super friendly service and a meal that transcends the concept of a basic burger – these things are epic. And lovely. Even the buns are baked onsite. There are veggie and vegan options too. The tunes are great and the boutique beer selection is comprehensive. Deservedly popular.

Cutler & Co.

55–57 Gertrude Street; tel: 9419 4888; www.cutlerandco.com.au; Tue–Sun 6pm–late, Fri and Sun noon–11pm; $$–$$$

This highly acclaimed restaurant by Andrew McConnell has received rave reviews from critics for its wow factor.

With a deft touch, the brutal surrounds of an old metalwork factory have been transformed into a stylish dining room and bar. The food, perfectly balanced in taste and texture, is simple, fresh and fabulous.

Ladro

224 Gertrude Street, Fitzroy; tel: 9415 7575; www.ladro.com.au, Sun noon–3pm, Mon–Fri 6–11pm, Sat–Sun 5.30–11pm; $

Melbourne's best pizza is on offer at this bustling and noisy place. The clientele matches the decor – arty chic – and eating here is very, very Melbourne. In winter the roasted meat of the day is popular, but most of the punters come for the thin-crust pizzas, topped with delights such as potato and truffle oil.

Moon Under Water

211 Gertrude Street, tel: 9417 7700; www.buildersarmshotel.com.au/moon-under-water; Tue–Sat 6–10pm; $$–$$$

Housed in Fitzroy's iconic Builders Arms Hotel, the Moon Under Water borrows its evocative name from a George Orwell essay. Everything else, though, is completely original, from the ultrawhite design by Projects of Imagination to the fare prepared by the formidable triumvirate of chefs, Andrew McConnell, Josh Murphy and Matthew Zaloum. There's no à la carte, instead you choose from 3-, 4- or 6-course kitchen menus, with vegetarian options available.

A big table at Hellenic Republic

Naked for Satan

285 Brunswick Street; tel: 94162238; www.nakedforsatan.com.au; Sun–Thur noon–midnight, Fri–Sat noon–1am; $–$$

An incredibly hip place serving Spanish Basque food in an old vodka distillery, decorated with photos of people in various stages of nudity – it doesn't get much more Brunswick than this. Back in the 1920s, a Russian émigré called Leon Satanovich busied himself with distilling vodka here – usually in the buff, apparently – hence the intriguing name. Come here for beers (12 on tap), and stay for the tapas, pintxo and sangria. The lunchtime deal is a steal. Check out the rooftop for the view (and to get an eyeful of the photos on the stairs). Wash it all down with a shot of infused vodka.

Vegie Bar

380 Brunswick Street; tel: 9417 6935; Mon–Thur 11am–10pm, Fri 11am–10.30pm, Sat 9am–10.30pm, Sun 9am–10pm; $

Whether you're a vegetarian or an open-minded carnivore, this very popular joint will sate your appetite with decent-sized plates of meat-free dishes that are as healthy as they are supremely tasty. The menu has been inspired by cuisines from all over the planet and the clientele is young and cosmopolitan.

The Yarra and Docklands

La Camera

Southgate, Southbank; tel: 9699 3600; www.lacamerasouthgate.com; Mon–Thur 7.30am–10.30pm, Fri 7.30am–late, Sat 8.30am–late, Sun 8.30am–10pm; $–$$

Perched in a peach of a spot on the banks of the Yarra, overlooking the more interesting end of town, La Camera has been serving cold beers and superb, unfussy Italian fare at an affordable price for well over 12 years. The atmosphere is relaxed, the service attentive and the people-watching opportunities are excellent.

Nine Elephants

67 Village Street, Docklands; tel: 03 9670 9909; Mon–Fri 11am–2.30pm and 5.30–10pm, Sat 5.30–10pm; $

Bringing some spice and personality to an area that needs a bit more of both, this eatery serves delicious and authentic Thai cooking with a smile. From the spicy seafood soup to the pad see-ew, via massaman curry and deep-fried rockling with tamarind sauce, the dishes are explosively flavoursome and very reasonably priced.

Nobu Melbourne

Crown Complex, 8 Whiteman Street, Southbank; tel: 9292 7879; www.nobu restaurants.com/melbourne; Mon–Thur noon–2.30pm. Fri–Sun noon–3pm, Sun–Thur 6–10.30pm, Fri–Sat 6–11pm; $$$$

Nobu's southern hemisphere outpost, just like the rest of this culinary empire, is a glamorous and vibrant affair. The modern Japanese menu follows the Nobu formula of great ingredients and flavours. Try the signature black cod

Nobu's sushi tacos

with miso or Nobu's creative version of fish and chips.

Prahran, South Yarra, Toorak and Windsor

David's

4 Cecil Place, Prahran; tel: 9529 5199; www.davidsrestaurant.com.au; Mon–Fri noon–3pm, Sat–Sun 11.30am–3pm, Sun–Thur 6–10.30pm, Fri–Sat 6–11pm; $–$$

David's is one of the more adventurous and interesting Chinese restaurants in town, championing food from Shanghai and tea with health-giving properties. Service is brisk and slurping is encouraged here – they take it as a compliment. There are banquet menus available for two people or more, a *yum cha* (dim sum) menu and an unusual array of tonic soups that (according to the restaurant) increase longevity and enhance libido and vitality. You can BYO (wine only) but there is a corkage charge of A$10 per bottle.

Bistro Gitan

52 Toorak Road West, South Yarra; tel: 9867 5853; www.bistrogitan.com.au; Mon and Sat 5pm–late, Tues–Fri noon–late; $$

Worldly wise wanderers who stumble across this contemporary bistro, named after the gypsy travellers of Europe, will instantly know they've found themselves a good thing. Housed in classic Victorian building opposite Fawkner Park, Gitan's revolving menu is heavily influenced by French and Spanish cuisine. It mixes quality with an endearing informality to recreate the ambience of a French family dinner table. Unsurprisingly, the wine list is c'est magnifique

Jacques Reymond

78 Williams Road, Windsor; tel: 9525 2178; www.jacquesreymond.com.au; Thur–Fri noon–1.30pm, Tue–Sat 6.30–9.30pm; $$$$

Vue de Monde may be more fashionable and decorated, but many local epicures prefer the restrained elegance and sophisticated execution of Jacques Reymond's food, which he has been serving from this suburban mansion for decades. Don't let this long pedigree fool you, though – Reymond is still one of the most innovative and exciting chefs in Australia, and a meal here is extremely hard to beat.

St Kilda and the Southeast

Attica

74 Glen Eira Road, Ripponlea; tel: 9530 0111; www.attica.com.au; Tue–Sat 6pm–8pm, $$$$

One of three Melbourne eateries boasting a prestigious three-hat rating, awarded by The Age, and also placed in illustrious company as one of the top 50 restaurants in the entire world, Attica is tucked away in the unassuming little suburb of Rippon Lea, but it's obviously well worth the trip (if you can get a table). Here, multi-award winning Kiwi chef Ben Shewry performs his magic, often employing unusual methods – potatoes baked in the earth, fish cooked in smoking paper bark. Clearly, though, it works.

Nobu Melbourne

Try the Chef's Table 5-course degustation menu on Tuesdays.

Big Mouth

168 Acland Street, St Kilda; tel: 9534 4611; www.bigmouthstkilda.com.au; Mon-Thurs noon–Late, Fri noon–3am, Sat 9am–3am, Sunday 9am–late; $-$$

Having stood loud and proud on the busy and boisterous corner of St Kilda's Barkly Street and Acland Street corner for over two decades, Big Mouth knows how to handle itself and meet the needs of its clientele. Downstairs is the place to sip wine and draft ales as you take big mouthfuls of mains like beef cheek, pork belly and confit duck, while upstairs is where a young crew graze on mezze and suck bottled beers.

Cerberus Beach House

Half Moon Bay, Black Rock; tel 9533 4028; www.cerberusbeachhouse.com.au; Tue–Thur noon–3pm and 5.30–10.30pm, Fri–Sat noon–3pm and 5.30–late, Sun 11.30am–3.30pm and 5.30–9.30pm; $$

You have to venture further around the Bay to find this gem, past the beautiful beachside suburbs of Brighton and Sandringham to Half Moon Bay at Black Rock. The upstairs restaurant is positioned beautifully, with views across the wreck of the HMAS Cerberus to the city skyline in the mid-distance. Come here for a sundowner and then tuck into the lovingly presented and supremely tasty main fare on offer, such as wagyu rump steak or spanner crab with gazpacho sauce. Or, grab some award-winning fish and chips and tuck into them as the tide tickles you toes on suburban Melbourne's best beach.

Claypots Seafood Restaurant

213 Barkly Street, St Kilda; tel: 9534 1282; noon–1am; $$

Serious, sensuous seafood – snapper, chilli crab, claws, mussels, oysters, octopus, you name it – served in steaming claypots and best enjoyed shared, with a beer or a glass of chilled white. BYO is allowed, and St Kilda's best bottleshop is just around the corner. This small, bustling restaurant, with a candlelit outside area, doesn't accept bookings. A very laid-back atmosphere prevails, and it's simply a matter of commandeering a whole table if you're in a big group, or pulling up a pew and rubbing elbows with fellow diners if there are only a couple of you.

Donovans

40 Jacka Boulevard; tel: 9534 8221; www.donovanshouse.com.au; daily noon–3pm, 6–10.30pm; $$$-$$$$

In late 2014, this historic restaurant – famous for its seafood and Italian dishes, as well as its unsurpassed view out over iconic St Kilda beach – suffered a devastating fire. Long-term proprietors Gail and Kevin Donovan have reassured traumatised regulars that they will be re-opening their doors in the summer of 2015.

Stokehouse's beachside balcony

Pizza e Birra

60a Fitzroy Street; tel: 9537 3465;
www.pizzaebirra.com.au; Tue–Fri noon–
3pm, Sun noon–4pm, Tue–Sat 6pm–late; $
The chef hails from Campania, so the pizzas served up here are of the thin-crust variety. They are a perfect match for the ice-cold beer provided on tap. Service is welcoming and the clientele is diverse, with families as much in evidence as glamorous 30something professionals.

Stokehouse

30 Jacka Boulevard; tel: 9525 5555;
www.stokehouse.com.au; daily noon–2pm
and 6–10pm; $$–$$$$
This is one of the first ports of call when Melburnians want to impress visitors from out of town. The downstairs bar serves pizza and fish and chips, and the upstairs restaurant, which has a superb view of the bay, offers a progressive menu using the freshest ingredients.

Richmond

Vlado's

61 Bridge Road, Richmond; tel: 9428 5833;
www.vlados.com.au; Mon–Fri noon–3pm
and 6pm–11pm, Sat 6–11pm; $$$$
Meat is the only thing that matters when you eat at Vlados – vegetarians should definitely avoid this place, but eyes-forward, bone-gnawing carnivores will absolutely love it. In terms of starters and side dishes, there's precious little choice, but when it comes to the main course a waiter will bring a selection of raw steaks to your table, solemnly request that you choose one, and ask how you would like it cooked. A few minutes later it will be melting in your mouth. 2014 marked the 50th year since this small family-owned restaurant first opened its doors, and its reputation as a steakhouse transcends anything else you will find in Melbourne.

Yarra Valley

Bella Vedere

874 Maroondah Highway, Coldstream;
tel: 5962 6161; www.bellavedere.com.au;
Wed–Sun 8.30am–5pm, Fri 6.30–10pm,
Sat 7.30–11pm; $$$
From the highway, this popular restaurant and cooking school in the Badger's Brook Estate doesn't promise much, but investigation pays off in spades. Inspiration for the menu comes courtesy of the huge vegetable and herb gardenand bread and pastries are baked fresh every day.

Great Ocean Road

Chill @ The Bay

14 Pascoe Street, Apollo Bay; tel:
52371006; daily 5.30–11pm; $–$$
A popular place serving fresh and lively Spanish-inspired fare to a happy hungry crowd of surfy types in Melbourne's favourite seaside town. Tuck into paella, churros, tapas and potato tortillas, then swig some home-made sangria to wash it down. DJs spin tunes later, and look out for happy hour deals.

NIGHTLIFE

Melbourne's bar scene is famous throughout Australia. Stylish drinking dens are located in obscure laneways throughout the city, and entertainment strips such as Brunswick, Gertrude and Chapel streets are full of edgy bars, pubs and clubs. You will never be bored in this city, no matter what day it is, or how late you're up.

Meanwhile, live music in Melbourne is very much in the air you breathe. There's a gig to catch in Melbourne almost every night, if you're not fussy about the genre of music. Many are underground venues or hidden in secluded spots, while others are perched on rooftops. A cardinal rule to remember: the cooler places are the more inconspicuous. For a great night out in the inner city, head to Brunswick Street, St Kilda or Prahran, which all have nightspots with resident and guest DJs. Some places open until dawn.

For an overview of the music, theatre, dance and film scenes, see page 20.

Central Melbourne

Bennetts Lane
25 Bennetts Lane; tel: 9663 2856; www.bennettslane.com; daily 8.30pm–late
The city's number-one jazz club, Bennetts Lane hosts local jazz luminaries and occasional high-profile international acts, such as Brad Mehldau. Though afi-cionados of the genre treat it like their local, it's an inclusive, attitude-free place.

Boney
68 Little Collins Street; tel: 9663 8268; www.boney.net.au; Mon–Wed noon–3am, Thur noon–5am, Fri-Sat noon–7am, Sun 5pm–5am
In the same party paddock where Melbourne's legendary dive bar Pony once played, Boney now cavorts. It's been cleaned up a bit, but this is still a haunt for the more serious night owls, with some acts in the bandroom not taking to the stage until 2am, and the bar staying open through to a bleary eyed 7am at the weekend. Food available until 7pm, after which the high jinx start for real.

The Carlton Hotel
Upstairs, 193 Bourke Street; tel: 9663 3216; www.thecarlton.com.au; Mon–Wed 3pm–late, Thur–Sun noon–late
Once a seedy pub, with a depressing interior and rough-as-guts clientele, the Carlton has had a makeover and is now packing Generation Ys in every night. The witty decor, excellent wine list, tasty bar snacks, art exhibitions and boisterous vibe make it a general fave.

Cherry Bar
AC/DC Lane, off Flinders Lane, between

A bouncer at the front door of the Cherry Bar in AC/DC Lane

Russell and Exhibition Streets; tel: 9639 8122; www.cherrybar.com.au; Mon 5pm–3am, Tue–Wed 6pm–3am, Thur–Sat 5pm–5am, Sun 2pm–3am

This legendary rock bar hit headlines in 2012 when it refused to accommodate megastar Lady Gaga's last minute request to stage her after-party in the venue, preferring to honour the commitment it had made to a local act instead. They earned major kudos for that, and Lady Gaga herself went straight there to party after her 2014 gig, so she was obviously impressed too. And so she should be – located on AC/DC lane (named after the notorious hard-living Australian rock act) and set up by former Cosmic Psychos drummer Bill Walsh, this late-night bar and live-music venue is so cool that Noel Gallagher once tried to buy it.

The Croft Institute

21-25 Croft Alley; tel: 9671 4399; www.thecroftinstitute.com; Mon–Thur 5pm–1am, Fri 5pm–3am, Sat 8pm–3am

Just finding this idiosyncratic place can be an adventure, but once you have located it, hidden away down a Chinatown alley, you've got three floors of curios to explore and bizarre thematic décor to sink your drink amid. Sip a test-tube cocktail in a science lab (try their revolving house concoction, the Experiment) and then head up to the beer- and gin-serving gym on the next level. Always weird, sometimes wonderful, very Mel-

bourne. On the top deck you'll find DJs spinning records during into the wee hours during the weekend.

Ding Dong Lounge

Floor 1, 18 Market Lane; tel: 03-9662 1020; www.dingdonglounge.com.au; Wed–Thur 7pm–3am, Fri–Sat 7pm–7am

Tucked away in the heart of Chinatown is Melbourne's underground and alternative rock 'n' roll bar, the cheeky Antipodean sister to New York City's Ding Dong Lounge. The club features DJs spinning a mix of classic and contemporary rock, new wave, electro, punk and garage.

Gin Palace

10 Russell Place; tel: 9654 0533; www.ginpalace.com.au; daily 4pm–3am

The seductive strains of lounge music and sound of cocktail shakers getting a workout greet you on entering this Melbourne institution. Its velvet-upholstered lounge chairs are claimed by a predominantly 30-something crowd, who are devoted to the bar's expertly concocted Martinis.

Melbourne Supper Club

161 Spring Street; tel: 9654 6300; www.theeuropean.com.au; Sun–Mon 8pm–4am, Tue–Thur 5pm–4am, Fri 5pm–6am, Sat 8pm–6am

Everyone loves the Melbourne Supper Club – upstairs at the European. In winter chesterfields and armchairs in the first-floor bar beckon; in sum-

mer the views from the terrace Siglo bar are so wonderful that it's hard to leave at the end of the evening. The wine list is exceptional, there's great food and the service is exemplary. See also page 36.

Meyers Place

20 Meyers Place; tel: 9650 8609; www.meyersplace.com.au; Mon–Thur 4pm–1am, Fri–Sat 4pm–4am

One of the first laneway bars in Melbourne, Meyers Place was started by a group of architects who wanted a place where they and their boho friends could enjoy a quiet drink after work. Near Parliament House, it has been joined in the lane by the equally popular **Loop** (23 Meyers Place; tel: 9654 0500; www.looponline.com.au; daily 3pm–late).

Seamstress

113 Lonsdale Street; tel: 9663 6363; www.seamstress.com.au; Mon–Tue, Sat 6pm–1am, Wed–Fri 11pm–1am

It's hip, it's hot and it's most definitely happening. There's a restaurant and a cocktail bar, as well as Sweatshop – another bar in the basement. They are as stylish as they come and have quickly endeared themselves to the city's barflies. The owners know their wine and cocktails, and match these with a tempting array of bar snacks, including Chinese dumplings, freshly shucked oysters and crispy rice balls.

Fitzroy

Black Pearl

304 Brunswick Street; tel: 9417 0455; www.blackpearlbar.com.au; Mon–Sun 5pm–3am

Chilled during the week, but wall-to-wall at weekends, this cocktail lounge manages to be trendy but unpretentious. Besides the mixologists' more colourful creations, the bar offers a choice of some 20 boutique beers by the bottle, and at least one revolving option on tap. Bar snacks do the rounds until 10pm, after which the drinking and schmoozing begins in earnest.

Builder's Arms Hotel

211 Gertrude Street; tel: 9419 0818; Mon–Thur 4pm–late, Fri–Sun 2pm–late

The Builder's Arms has been reinvented since Andrew McConnell took it over – it now has two top-class eateries under its roof, a monkey in the upstairs window and far fewer actual builders resting their arms on the bar – but, if you don't mind rubbing elbows with bearded hipsters, this is still a drinking den of sorts. Particularly if you like your craft beers served on tap, because there's an impressive 10-strong selection of these, including local heroes Mountain Goat, Vale and 4 Pines.

The Union Club Hotel

164 Gore Street; tel: 9417 2926; www.unionclubhotel.com.au; Mon–Wed:

In the famed Prince Bandroom

3pm–late, Thur–Sun noon–late

While many of old Fitzroy's watering holes have morphed into posh eating joints (see the aforementioned Builder's Arms), the Union on the corner of Gore and Webb Streets remains a solid pub – complete with pool table, open fire, beer garden and footy on the TV. Food is available, and it's good, but this is an excellent option for an ale under the garden fig tree, or up on the roof deck, in the company of the bright young things of Fitzroy.

Prahran, South Yarra and Toorak

Revolver Upstairs

229 Chapel Street, Prahran;
www.revolverupstairs.com.au;
tel: 9521 5985; Mon–Thur noon–4am,
Fri–Sun 24hr

Local and international DJs and bands take pride of place here at this long-running, late-opening, hard-partying stubbornly alternative venue in the heart of Chapel Street, but there are also record launches, indie film screenings and art exhibitions. Never a dull moment. Check the website to see what's on.

St Kilda and Elsternwick

George Lane Bar

1 George Lane (off Grey Street); tel: 9593 8884; www.georgelanebar.com.au; Wed–Fri 6pm–1am, Sat–Sun 7pm–1am

In a laneway behind the landmark George Hotel, this popular bar can't accommodate many drinkers, but those who do score a spot here always leave happy. There's a refreshingly laid-back vibe and a DJ at weekends. The nearby **George Public Bar** (located in the basement of the George Hotel, 127 Fitzroy Street; tel: 9534 8822) is a popular place to shoot some pool and sink some pots.

Prince Bandroom

29 Fitzroy Street; tel: 9536 1168;
www.princebandroom.com.au

One of Melbourne's most famous live-music venues, the Prince has a leafy balcony overlooking Fitzroy Street and an atmosphere-packed downstairs bar (much less rough than it once was). Acts are as diverse as the clientele, harking from both Australia and overseas, and have included Lenny Kravitz, Scissor Sisters, Pink, Coldplay and Bright Eyes.

Flying Saucer Club

4 St Georges Road, Elsternwick; tel: 9528 3600; www.flyingsaucerclub.com.au;
Mon–Fri food 6–8pm, performances 8pm, Sat–Sun doors open 3pm

A relatively new name on Melbourne's night scene, the Flying Saucer Club has landed in a bohemian hood close to Elsternwick train station, where it serves up a smorgasbord of contemporary music, cabaret, spoken word, burlesque, comedy and musical theatre. Food is served prior to performances.

A–Z

A

Age restrictions

The age of consent for both heterosexual and homosexual sex in Victoria is 16. Drivers must be aged 18 to obtain a licence. To drink or buy alcohol, or smoke any tobacco product, people must be at least 18 years old.

B

Budgeting

Accommodation. A bed at a backpacker hostel costs fromaround A$25 a night, a room in a three-star hotel costs about A$150 and a room in a four- or five-star hotel can start as low as A$200.

Restaurants. A main course costs around A$20 at a budget restaurant, A$25–30 at a mid-range restaurant and over A$40 at an expensive restaurant. A 285ml glass of beer (a 'pot') costs around A$5–6 and a cup of tea or coffee is about A$3.50. A glass of house wine averages around A$8–10 in most bars and restaurants.

Car rental. Renting a small car starts at A$50 per day including taxes. Petrol (gasoline) is more expensive than in the US, but is considerably cheaper than in most European countries. Many cars take diesel – check before you fill up.

Airport taxi. A taxi between Melbourne Airport and central Melbourne will cost around A$55.

See Melbourne Attractions Pass. This gives the holder admission to more than 30 attractions in Melbourne as well as the surrounding regions. The card comes in two-, three- and seven-day versions, and can be purchased online (http://seemelbourne pass.iventurecard.com) or at the Melbourne Visitor Centre at Federation Square.

C

Clothing

'Four seasons in one day' is a statement regularly used to describe Melbourne's weather. Be ready for any conditions at any time; a warm sweater is often needed in summer, and winter can call for heavy jackets, scarves and gloves – but can also throw sudden warm sunny days at you. It's not a bad idea to carry an umbrella not matter what time of year it is. Definitely have access to a raincoat from April to September, and wear sunblock and a hat for summer.

Crime and safety

Although Melbourne has a reputation as being a friendly and safe place in which to live and travel, you should

Aerial view of the CBD

use the same common sense and precautions as you would elsewhere regarding your possessions and personal security. The nightclub precinct in central Melbourne (especially around King Street) and the area around the railway station platforms in the city centre and suburbs can be dangerous late at night, when excessive alcohol consumption sometimes triggers violent incidents.

Customs

Australia has extremely strict regulations about what can and cannot be brought into the country. Before disembarking from a plane, visitors are asked to fill in an Incoming Passenger Card. Australian customs officers check the information on the cards when passengers disembark and may initiate a baggage search. Sniffer dogs also patrol, giving bags the once over. There are heavy fines for false or inaccurate claims, so it is always best to declare an item if in doubt – items of interest to officials include dirty walking boots or trainers, and don't try and bring any fruit in, even if it was given to you on the plane. In addition, there are strict quarantine rules when entering and travelling between states.

Anyone over the age of 18 is allowed to bring into Australia A$900 worth of goods (not including alcohol or tobacco), 2,250ml (about 4 pints) of alcohol (wine, beer or spirits) and 250 cigarettes or 250g of cigars or tobacco products other than cigarettes. These regulations are liable to change, for more information, see www.customs.gov.au.

Disabled travellers

The **National Information Communications Awareness Network** (NICAN; tel: 1800 806 769; www.nican.com.au) is a national organisation that keeps an online database of facilities and services with access for the disabled, including accommodation and tourist sights.

Low-floor trams and buses suitable for wheelchairs are gradually being introduced to Melbourne's public transport system. For details of accessible stops and services, go to www.transport.vic.gov.au/doi/internet/transport.nsf and click on the Accessibility of Public Transport link.

The **Melbourne Mobility Centre** (1st Floor, Federation Square Car Park, corner Russell and Flinders streets; tel: 1800 735 266, National Relay Service: call 133 677 and ask for 03 9658 9658; www.accessmelbourne.vic.gov.au; Mon–Fri 9am–6pm, Sat–Sun 10am–4pm) offers services such as wheelchair hire, information for visitors with disabilities, fully accessible toilets and National Relay Service.

There are **Travellers Aid Centres** (tel: 9654 2600; www.travellersaid.org.

Part of the Federation Tapestry in the Melbourne Museum

au) at the Flinders Street and Southern Cross stations. These offer accessible toilets with hoist and adult change tables, toileting assistance, wheelchair hire and recharging, and communication assistance.

Most of the large tourist attractions are wheelchair-accessible.

E

Electricity

The current is 240/250v, 50Hz, and Australia uses 'type I' plugs with a grounding pin and two flat prongs forming a V shape. Most hotels have universal outlets for 110v shavers and small appliances.

Embassies and consulates

British Consulate General, 17th Floor, 90 Collins Street, Melbourne 3000; tel: 9652 1600 (office hours); http://ukin australia.fco.gov.uk; Mon–Fri 10am– 12.30pm and 1.30–4pm.

Visa and passport enquiries should be made to the British High Commission in Canberra: Commonwealth Avenue, Yarralumla, ACT 2600; tel: 1902 941 555; Mon–Fri 9am–5pm.

Consulate of Canada, Level 27, 101 Collins Street, Melbourne (by appointment); tel: 9653 9674; www.canada. org.au.

Visa and passport enquiries should be made to the **Consulate General of Canada**: Level 5, 111 Harrington Street, Sydney, NSW 2000; tel: 02-9364 3000;

Mon–Fri 8.30am–4.30pm.
Embassy of Ireland, 20 Arkana Street, Yarralumla, ACT 2600, Canberra; tel: 02-6214 0000; www.embassyofireland. au.com; Mon–Thur 9.30am–12.45pm and 2–5pm, Fri 2–4pm.
Consulate General of the United States, 553 St Kilda Road, Melbourne 3004; tel: 9526 5900; http://mel bourne.usconsulate.gov; Mon–Fri 9am– 4pm.

Emergencies

For police, fire or ambulance, call 000. From a mobile phone, try calling 112 if you are having trouble getting reception or signal (this is a secondary emergency number, available from all GSM or GSM derived mobile phones, which works all over the world and will automatically default to the national emergency service closest to you)– or 106, which connects to the text-based relay service for people who have a hearing or speech impairment.

G

Gay and lesbian travellers

Melbourne has a thriving gay scene. Clubs and bars are clustered in the inner-northern suburbs of Fitzroy, Collingwood, Abbotsford and Prahran. The suburb of Northcote, in the inner north, has a large lesbian community, and the suburbs of South Yarra, Prahran and St Kilda in the inner south are favoured by gay men.

The Australian and The Financial Review are Australia's two national dailies

To find out what's on in the city, pick up a copy of the free weekly publication *Melbourne Community Voice* (www.gaynewsnetwork.com.au) in cafés and bars around town. Alternatively, tune into JOY (94.9 FM), Melbourne's radio station for the gay, lesbian, bisexual, transgender and intersex community.

Each year, the Midsumma Festival (www.midsumma.org.au) celebrates gay culture through arts and sporting events, dance parties and a Pride March.

Gay and Lesbian Tourism Australia (www.galta.com.au) promotes gay-owned or gay-friendly accommodation and tour operators via its website.

Green issues

Victorians take environmental issues very seriously – in state elections at the end of 2014, history was made when Ellen Sandell became the first state MP for the Greens after winning victory in seat of Melbourne –and each of the three tiers of government offers programmes and services to foster environmentally responsible behaviour. Due to the nationwide drought, water restrictions have been in place across the state since 2005 – when here, take short showers and don't leave taps running. Recycling of glass, plastic, aluminium and paper is widespread – look for recycling bins with yellow lids. For more information, see www.sustainability.vic.gov.au.

All travellers should be aware that flying produces a huge amount of carbon dioxide and is a significant contributor to global warming. If you would like to offset the damage caused to the environment by your flight, a number of organisations can do this for you using on-line 'carbon calculators' that tell you how much you need to donate. In the UK travellers can visit www.climatecare.org or www.carbonneutral.com; in the US log on to www.climatefriendly.com or www.sustainabletravel.org.

Health

Australia has excellent medical services. For medical attention outside of working hours, go to the casualty department of a major hospital, look for a medical practitioner in the *Yellow Pages* (www.yellow-pages.com.au) or ask at your hotel for advice.

The biggest danger for travellers in Australia is the sun. Even on mild, cloudy days it has the potential to burn. Wear a broad-brimmed hat and a long-sleeved shirt made from a light fabric when spending extended periods of time in the sun, and a spray top when snorkelling or swimming. It is recommended that you wear SPF30+ sunblock at all times, even under a hat.

Inoculations. No vaccinations are required for entry to Australia.

Health care and insurance. The Australian Government has signed Recip-

rocal Health Care Agreements with the governments of the Republic of Ireland and New Zealand, which entitle citizens of those countries to limited subsidised health services for medically necessary treatment while visiting Australia.

If you are a citizen of the United Kingdom you are entitled to the same limited subsidised health services for medically necessary treatment, and you are also entitled to Medicare benefits for out-of-hospital medical treatment provided by doctors through private surgeries and community health centres. Visitors from all other countries should organise their own private medical insurance.

Pharmacies and hospitals. The chemist (pharmacy) is a great place to go for advice on minor ailments such as bites, rashes and stomach troubles. If you have a prescription from your doctor at home, and you want to take it to a pharmacist in Australia, you will need to have it endorsed by a local medical practitioner.

Hours and holidays

Shops usually open 9am to 5pm Monday to Friday(often later) and weekends from 10am to 5pm. Late-night shopping occurs in the CBD on Thursdays and Fridays, with most stores open until 7pm or 9pm.

Public holidays

1 January: New Year's Day
26 January: Australia Day/Invasion Day
2nd Monday in March: Labour Day
March/April: Good Friday, Easter Saturday and Monday
25 April: Anzac Day
2nd Monday in June: Queen's Birthday
1st Tuesday in November: Melbourne Cup
25 December: Christmas Day
26 December: Boxing Day
When a public holiday falls on a weekend, the following Monday is declared a holiday.

L

Left luggage

Travellers Aid (Main Concourse, Flinders Street Station, Flinders and Swanston streets, between platforms 9 and 10; tel: 9610 2030; www.travellers aid.org.au; Sun–Thur 8am–8pm, Fri–Sat 8am–10pm) offers short-term luggage storage at reasonable rates. More expensive luggage lockers are available at **Southern Cross Railway Station** (tel: 9619 2588; www.southerncross station.net.au; open during train service times). At the airport, luggage storage is offered by **SmarteCarte** (daily 5am–12.30am), in the Arrivals Hall in Terminal 2.

Lost property

The loss or theft of valuables should be reported to the police immediately, as most insurance policies insist

Webb Footbridge across the Yarra

on a police report. To do this, call the non-emergency telephone number, 9247 6666. For property lost on the major airlines or bus and coach services, try the following numbers:

Melbourne International Airport, tel: 9297 1805; Qantas Baggage Services, tel: 1300 306 980 or 8336 4100; Jetstar Baggage Services, tel: 1800 687 374; Virgin Australia, tel: 8346 2437 (international), 9339 1750 (domestic); Southern Cross Station Luggage Hall, tel: 9619 2588; Metro (trains), tel: 1800 696 3876; Yarra Trams, tel: 1800 800 166.

M

Maps

The Melbourne Visitor Centre at Federation Square stocks the free *Melbourne Official Visitors' Map*, covering the central city and the train and tram networks, plus free maps of regional Victoria. PDFs of transport maps are available at http://ptv.vic.gov.au/getting-around/maps.

The *Insight Guides Fleximap: Melbourne* is a handy, laminated map that won't break in the rain.

Media

Print media. The city's major broadsheet is *The Age* (www.theage.com.au); tabloid readers opt for the *Herald Sun* (www.heraldsun.com.au). The two national dailies are *The Australian* (www.theaustralian.com.au)

and the *Financial Review* (www.afr.com). The city's free street press titles include *Beat* (www.beat.com.au) and *Inpress* (www.themusic.com.au), both good for entertainment listings. You can pick these up at pubs, cafés and music stores.

Radio and television. The Australian Broadcasting Corporation (ABC) runs four national television channels as well as an extensive network of local and national radio stations, including Radio National (621 AM) and Melbourne-based 3LO (774 AM). Both offer excellent current affairs programmes and talkback. There's also Triple J (107.5 FM) for alternative music and Classic FM (105.9 FM).

Three commercial television broadcasters (Ten, Nine and Seven) offer news, drama, soaps and game shows, heavily punctuated with adverts.

Australia's free-to-air ethnic/multicultural broadcaster, SBS, offers many foreign-language films and documentaries, foreign news, international football (soccer) and Australia's best world news. SBS Radio (93.1 FM or 1224 AM) broadcasts programmes in a wide variety of languages.

Local community radio stations 3RRR (102.7 FM) and PBS (106.7 FM) have devoted followings and feature a lot of excellent local content. Both are superb windows into Melbourne's independent soul.

Internet facilities. Most Victorian households have internet access at

Chinese New Year sees the whole of Chinatown come alive with performances, ceremonies and fireworks

home, and – with an increasing number of travellers carrying their own laptops, tablets or smartphones, and a plethora of cafes, pubs, hotels and hostels offering free Wifi – there are very few internet cafés around these days. The State Library of Victoria offers free internet access on 50 PCs in the second-floor Redmond Barry Reading Room (60-minute maximum) and on 50 PCs in the ground-floor Information Centre (15-minute maximum). The library also offers free WiFi.

Money

Banks. The five major banks are anz, Commonwealth, National Australia Bank, Westpac and Bendigo Bank. Trading hours are generally 9am to 4pm Monday to Thursday, and 9am–5pm Friday. Some branches open on Saturday mornings.

Currency. The local currency is the Australian dollar (abbreviated as AUD$, A$ or simply $), made up of 100 cents. There are 5c, 10c, 20c, 50c, $1 and $2 coins and $5, $10, $20, $50 and $100 notes. Single cents are still applied to many prices, and in these cases the amount will be rounded down or up to the nearest 5c.

Credit cards. Visa and MasterCard are accepted almost everywhere; American Express and Diners Club aren't quite as welcome.

Cash machines. Bank branches and automatic teller machines (ATMs) are common throughout Melbourne. ATMs are 24hr and are linked with Cirrus, Maestro, Barclays and other networks, meaning that you can use them to access funds from overseas accounts.

Traveller's cheques. All well-known traveller's cheques can be exchanged for cash at banks, five-star hotels and exchange bureaux.

Tipping. Tipping is not obligatory, but a small gratuity for good service will be appreciated. When paying for a taxi fare, it is customary to round up to the nearest dollar or two. Restaurants do not usually levy a service charge, so most people tip waiters 10 per cent of the bill for good service. Hotel porters will expect between A$2–5, depending on how much baggage you have.

Taxes. A 10 percent Goods and Services Tax (GST) is automatically added to most purchases. Visitors who purchase goods with a total value of A$300 or more from any one accredited supplier within 30 days of their departure from Australia are entitled to a refund under the Tourist Refund Scheme (TRS). Refunds can be claimed at the TRS booth located beyond customs at the airport. For more details, see www. customs.gov.au.

Police

In an emergency, call 000. At other times call the general enquiries number for **Victoria Police** (tel: 9247 6666; Mon–Fri 7am–7pm). There are two

police stations in central Melbourne that are open 24 hours: **Melbourne East** (tel: 9637 1100; 226 Flinders Lane) and **Melbourne West** (tel: 9247 6491; 637 Flinders Street).

Post

The efficient – but expensive – postal system is operated by **Australia Post** (tel: 13 7678; www.auspost.com.au), a government-run business enterprise that franchises its storefront operations. Post offices are generally open 9am to 5pm Monday to Friday. There are a number of post offices in the CBD, including at 250 and 410 Elizabeth Street, 246 Flinders Lane, 210 Lonsdale Street and 440 Collins Street.

You can buy stamps at all post offices and at some newsagents. For assured next-day delivery within Australia it is possible to buy special Express Post envelopes. Otherwise, mail takes between one and three days to be delivered.

The cost of overseas mail depends on the weight and size of the item. At the time of writing, it costs A$2.75 to send a postcard or letter weighing up to 50g. Standard overseas mail takes about a week to most destinations.

Post boxes are red (standard mail) and yellow (Express Post mail).

Smoking

It is illegal to smoke inside restaurants, bars, pubs and clubs in Victoria. Many venues have outdoor areas where smoking is allowed. It is also illegal to smoke on covered train platforms and in bus and tram shelters.

Telephones

The national code for Australia is 61 and the area code for Victoria is 03.

To call out of Australia, dial 0011 + country code + area code (drop the first 0) + main number. The country code for Ireland is 353, the UK is 44 and for the US and Canada dial 1.

Public phones. In the era of the ubiquitous mobile phone landlines are becoming ever rarer, but you can usually find public phones located outside post offices and major transport terminals in the CBD, as well as in many pubs. These operate with coins and (increasingly) phonecards; the latter are sold through newsagents, post offices and Telstra shops, and can be used to make interstate and international calls.

Mobile phones. All Australian mobile numbers have a four-digit prefix starting with 04. To use your mobile (cell) here, buy a local SIM card and top it up with prepaid calls. Providers include Virgin Mobile (www.virgin mobile.com.au), Telstra (www.telstra. com), Optus (www.optus.com.au) and Vodafone (www.vodafone.com.au). All have shops in the CBD.

Melbourne's taxis are yellow

Time zones

Melbourne is on Eastern Australian Standard Time (EST), which is 10 hours ahead of Greenwich Mean Time (GMT) and between 14 and 16 hours ahead of New York (according to the time of year). For travellers, things get complicated when you factor in Daylight Saving (when the clocks in parts of Australia and the US go forward by an hour) and British Summer time (when clocks in the UK go forward by an hour). So, when it is noon in Melbourne outside of Daylight Saving, it is 2am according to Greenwich Mean Time (but 3am in London during British Summer time) and 10pm (the previous day) in New York.

Daylight Saving operates from the start of October to the start of April in Victoria (which roughly corresponds to the period when the UK reverts to GMT and New York drops Daylight Saving), and during this period, Melbourne is 11 hours ahead of London and 16 ahead of New York, meaning when it's noon in Melbourne, it's 1am in London and 8pm (the previous day) in New York.

Toilets

There are pay toilets in some CBD streets, but most locals take advantage of the free toilets in the Myer and David Jones department stores in the Bourke Street Mall, in pubs, at railway stations and in large fast-food restaurants. The department store toilets also offer baby-change tables.

Tourist information

For online information, go to the Tourism Victoria websites: www.visitvictoria.com and www.visitmelbourne.com. It is also worth checking the Melbourne City Council tourism website: www.thatsmelbourne.com.au.

The extremely helpful **Melbourne Visitor Centre** (tel: 9658 9658; daily 9am–6pm) is located at the northwestern corner of Federation Square. There is also a **Melbourne Visitor Booth** (Mon–Sat 9am–5pm, Sun 10am–5pm) in the Bourke Street Mall.

Red-jacketed volunteers known as City Ambassadors can be found on the streets from Monday to Saturday. They can help with directions, transport queries and tourism information.

Transport

The vast majority of visitors to Victoria arrive by air. But once in Melbourne, there are plenty of ways to get around.

Airports and arrival

There are two airports: **Tullamarine International Airport** (Melbourne International; tel: 9297 1600; www.melbourneairport.com.au), which is 22km (14 miles) northwest of the city centre, and the much smaller **Avalon Airport** (tel: 1800 282 566; www.avalonairport.com.au), 55km (34 miles) southwest of the city centre on the road to Geelong.

Surprisingly, for a modern city such as Melbourne, there is no rail link to either airport.

A taxi to or from the international airport takes 20–30 minutes and costs upwards of A$55 from the city centre. To Avalon, the trip takes around 50 minutes and costs around A$130 (bear this in mind when booking tickets to other cities).

Skybus (tel: 9335 2811; www.sky bus.com.au; adult A$18 one way, A$30 return) operates a daily 24-hour shuttle bus service between the Melbourne Airport and Southern Cross Railway Station. Buses depart every 10 minutes during the day and every 15–30 minutes overnight. It also offers a pick-up/drop-off service to city hotels. All you have to do is transfer onto a SkyBus Hotel Transfer mini-bus at Southern Cross station, after registering your hotel details at the Hotel Transfer booth.

Sita Coaches (tel: 9689 7999; www. sitacoaches.com.au/avalon; A$22 one way, A$42 return) offers a shuttle bus service meeting all arriving and departing Jetstar and Tiger Airways flights at Avalon Airport. The bus drops passengers at Southern Cross Station or at city hotels (extra charge levied and online booking essential).

Public transport

Melbourne's integrated public transport system is run by **Metlink** (tel: 131 638; www.metlinkmelbourne.com.au) and comprises trams, buses and trains.

A good way to introduce yourself to its services and buy tickets is to visit the **MetShop** (Mon–Fri 9am–5.30pm, Sat 9am–1pm) on the ground floor of the Melbourne Town Hall, on the corner of Swanston and Little Collins streets.

The touch-on and touch-off ticketing system used in metropolitan Melbourne is called **myki**, and visitors must get their heads around how this works, as paper tickets have been phased out in the metro region. Fortunately, it's not rocket science – although the official websites aren't particularly easy to navigate. Basically, if you are going to be travelling around Melbourne for 7 days or more, purchase a reusable card (A$6), put some credit on it (per week for zone 1 A$35.80), touch it against the readers when you enter or leave a station/tram/bus, and top it up when required. The daily rate of travelling around Zone 1 like this works out as A$5.11 (unlimited number of trips for that day). If you're going to be in the city for a shorter period of time, use myki money, a 'pay as you go' method of purchasing 2-hour (A$3.58 for zone 1) and daily fares ($7.16 for zone 1 on a weekday, A$6 at weekends).

You can buy a myki and charge/recharge it at stations and selected some tram stops and bus interchanges, plus 800 retail outlets, including all 7-Eleven stores, as well as online. Note, these tickets can only be used on metro services, and are valid on trains, trams and buses

(excluding the airport bus and any other privately operated special service). Concessions are available for children aged 14 and under, and to holders of an approved Victorian Concession Card. For more, see http://ptv.vic.gov.au/tickets/myki.

Free city transport

The free City Circle tram operates in both directions around the outer edge of the CBD (including along Spring, La Trobe and Flinders streets). Old 'W'-class trams painted brown to be different to other services, they stop at the Docklands and close to major tourist attractions including Federation Square, Melbourne Aquarium and the Melbourne Museum.

The Melbourne City Tourist Shuttle is a free bus service that stops at key tourist attractions in and around the City of Melbourne. Find out more at www.thats melbourne.com.au/shuttle.

Taxis

You can hail one of Melbourne's yellow-coloured taxis in the street if its rooftop light is on. Alternatively, taxi ranks can be found at major hotels or busy locations such as train stations. A trip from one end of the CBD to the other costs around A$10. There are surcharges for phone bookings, and for trips between midnight and 5am, departing from the airport taxi rank and using the CityLink freeway or other tolls.

The major companies are **Silver Top Taxis** (tel: 131 008; www.silvertop.com. au) and **13 CABS** (aka Black Cabs, tel: 132 227; www.13cabs.com.au).

Note: in Melbourne it is compulsory to pay taxi fares upfront between the hours of 10pm and 5am. You can access a standard fare calculator online: www.taxifare.com.au.

Driving

All road traffic drives on the left in Australia. Most of Victoria's road regulations are based on international rules, and it is simply a matter of following the signs and sticking to the speed limits. Vic Roads (www.vicroads.vic.gov.au) can provide information about road rules.

The speed limit in built-up city and suburban areas is 40kph (25mph), 50kph (30mph) or 60kph (38mph). On country roads it is 100kph (60mph) unless otherwise indicated. Look out for dramatically reduced speed limits around schools at certain times of the day during the week. Speed cameras are common, and they are cunningly concealed.

There is a 0.05 per cent blood alcohol limit for drivers, which is widely enforced by the use of random breath tests carried out by the police – during which entire roads can be cordoned off. Random drug tests are also used.

Car rental. To rent a car for excursions into regional Victoria, you must be over 25 and possess a full licence in your

Melbourne tram

country of origin. You will need a copy of the licence in English or an International Driving permit, your passport and a credit card to which a pre-authorised security bond can be charged. Drivers between 18 and 25 may be able to hire a vehicle if they pay a surcharge.

Car-rental firms with offices in central Melbourne and desks at the airports include **Avis** (tel: 136 333; www.avis. com.au), **Budget** (tel: 1300 362 848; www.budget.com.au), **Europcar** (tel: 1300 131 390; www.europcar.com.au) and **Thrifty** (tel: 1300 367 227; www. thrifty.com.au).

Car parks. There are many multi-storey car parks in the CBD, as well as street parking. Parking inspectors are very diligent about ticketing cars whose meters have expired, and will hammer you if you park in an illegal spot (some busy roads have a tow-away policy for offenders, and it is very expensive to get your car back).

Cycling

Melbourne is fairly flat, which affords the cyclist a number of good long tracks. Bike paths lie along the Yarra River, the Maribyrnong and the Merri Creek. For general cycling information, contact **Bicycle Network Victoria** at 4/246 Bourke Street, tel: 03-8636 8888; www.bv.com.au.

Melbourne Bike Share (www.melbournebikeshare.com.au) has docking stations around the city and, for a small fee, bikes are available for sightseeing.

Helmets are compulsory, however, so go equipped or buy a cheap one from a local store. You can also download a related map and app to help you check bike and bike dock availability near you.

Visas and passports

Foreign nationals entering Australia must have a passport valid for the entire period of their stay and must have obtained a visa before leaving home (except for New Zealand citizens, who are issued with a visa on arrival in Australia). The Electronic Transfer Authority (ETA) visa is available to citizens of over 30 countries and can be obtained on the spot from travel agents or airline offices for a service charge of A$20. ETA visas are generally valid for 12 months; single stays must not exceed three months, but return visits within the 12-month period are allowed.

Most EU citizens are eligible for an eVisitor visa, which is free and can be obtained online.

Tourist visas are available for citizens of all countries for continuous stays of three, six or 12 months. You can apply for one of these online; a charge may be levied whether your application is successful or not.

Visitors travelling on ETAs, eVisitor visas and tourist visas are not permitted to work while in Australia.

For more information and to apply for visas online, go to www.immi.gov.au.

Eric Bana in 'Chopper'

BOOKS AND FILM

Melburnians have a highly developed appreciation of art and culture, and the city has a thriving community of filmmakers and writers. In 2008 Melbourne was named by UNESCO as a 'City of Literature', then only the second city to ever be awarded this honour, after Edinburgh in Scotland.

Books

Melbourne boasts the largest literary publishing sector in Australia, and has more independent bookshops and readers than anywhere else in the country. It hosts a range of literary festivals, including the Melbourne Writers' Festival and the Emerging Writers' Festival, and the excellent Australian literary magazine *Kill Your Darlings* was born here in 2010.

Two of Australia's foremost 19th-century novelists, **Rolf Boldrewood** (aka Thomas Browne, author of *Robbery Under Arms*) and **Marcus Clarke** (*For the Term of His Natural Life*), lived in Melbourne. **C.J. Dennis** (*Songs of a Sentimental Bloke*) was the most famous of the city's early poets. *The Getting of Wisdom* by **Henry Handel Richardson**, an Australian classic, is a coming-of-age novel set in late 19th-century Victoria, largely based on the real life of Ethel Lindesay (the author behind the pseudonym).

Australia's best-known author, **Peter Carey**, was born and raised just outside Melbourne, in Bacchus Marsh, and studied at the city's Monash University. Carey is one of only three writers to be awarded the Man Booker Prize twice – for *Oscar and Lucinda* (1988) and *The True History of the Kelly Gang* (2001), and he has thrice won the Miles Franklin Award.

Internationally admired musician, **Nick Cave**, is a Melburnian, and has turned his dark pen to two, very different novels: the complex southern Gothic classic *And the Ass Saw the Angel* (1988) and the more accessible (but no less disturbing) *The Death of Bunny Munro* (2009).

Tony Birch – a writer from Melbourne whose background is part Aborigine, part West Indian and part Irish – has won considerable acclaim for his poetry, short stories and novels, which include *Blood* (2011). **Rodd Moss**, an artist and author from Melbourne, won the 2011 Prime Minister's Award for Non Fiction for his heartbreaking and vivid portrait of Aboriginal life in modern Australia, *The Hard Light of Day*.

Non-fiction books that paint a picture of Melbourne through the decades include *My Brother Jack* by **George Johnston**, and *Unpolished Gem* by **Alice Pung**, who grew up in Footscray after escaping Pol Pot's Cambodia. *My Life As Me* by **Barry Humphreys** is a hilarious reminiscence of growing up in 1950s Melbourne by the man behind

The poster for 'Animal Kingdom'

Dame Edna Everage.

Steven Carroll won the Miles Franklin Award and the Commonwealth Writers' Prize for *The Time We Have Taken* and was shortlisted for various awards for *The Art of the Engine Driver* and *The Gift of Speed*.

Melbourne is also one of the world's leading cities for children's literature and acclaimed writers include **Wendy Orr** (*Nim's Island*), **Graeme Base** (*Animalia*) and **Andy Griffiths** (*The Day My Bum Went Psycho*). The most famous Australian children's book ever produced, *The Magic Pudding* (1918), was written by **Norman Lindsay**, from Creswick, a Victorian town 129km northwest of Melbourne. Lindsay worked in Melbourne on a local magazine, and wrote about his experiences in the city in *Rooms and Houses*.

Prolific local author **Sonya Hartnett** was first published when she was 13. Her award-winning titles – typically described as young adult fiction – include *Sleeping Dogs* and *Thursday's Child*, but the sexually explicit *Landscape with Animals* caused some controversy when it was published under a pseudonym in 2006.

Film

Melbourne has a thriving independent cinema scene and the work of indie filmmakers is comprehensively covered on the website www.innersense.com.au/mif.

Many mainstream movies have been shot in Melbourne, from *On The Beach* (1957) to *Where the Wild Things Are* (2009). Melbourne also provided the backdrop for TV series *The Pacific* (2010), produced by **Steven Spielberg** and starring **Tom Hanks**.

The city has produced and nurtured numerous big-name actors, including **Cate Blanchett**, who has won two Oscars for her performances in *The Aviator* (2004) and *Blue Jasmine* (2013).

Eric Bana, star of many Hollywood blockbusters, started out as a stand-up comedian in Melbourne, but his film breakthrough came with an exceptional lead performance in *Chopper* (2000), a film about real-life criminal Mark 'Chopper' Read, set and filmed around Melbourne. The city's criminal underbelly is also the subject of the critically acclaimed 2010 film *Animal Kingdom*.

Russell Crowe's early roles include a stint staring in the perennially popular Melbourne-based soap *Neighbours*, and his breakthrough performance was in *Romper Stomper*, a well-regarded film about skinheads in suburban Melbourne. **Guy Pearce**, his *LA Confidential* co-star (*Memento*, *Priscilla Queen of the Desert*, *The King's Speech*) was brought up Geelong and also started out in *Neighbours*.

Nicole Kidman studied at the Victorian College of the Arts in Melbourne, and Geoffrey Rush lives in the Melbourne suburb of Camberwell. Other notable actors who hail from Melbourne include **Rachel Griffiths** and **Radha Mitchell**, as well as the up-and-coming actors, brothers **Chris** and **Liam Hemsworth**.

ABOUT THIS BOOK

This *Explore Guide* has been produced by the editors of Insight Guides, whose books have set the standard for visual travel guides since 1970. With top-quality photography and authoritative recommendations, these guidebooks bring you the very best routes and itineraries in the world's most exciting destinations.

BEST ROUTES

The routes in the book provide something to suit all budgets, tastes and trip lengths. As well as covering the destination's many classic attractions, the itineraries track lesser-known sights, and there are also excursions for those who want to extend their visit outside the city. The routes embrace a range of interests, so whether you are an art fan, a gourmet, a history buff or have kids to entertain, you will find an option to suit.

We recommend reading the whole of a route before setting out. This should help you to familiarise yourself with it and enable you to plan where to stop for refreshments – options are shown in the 'Food and Drink' box at the end of each tour.

For our pick of the tours by theme, consult Recommended Routes for... (see pages 4 – 5).

INTRODUCTION

The routes are set in context by this introductory section, giving an overview of the destination to set the scene, plus background information on food and drink, shopping and more, while a succinct history timeline highlights the key events over the centuries.

DIRECTORY

Also supporting the routes is a Directory chapter, with a clearly organised A – Z of practical information, our pick of where to stay while you are there and select restaurant listings; these eateries complement the more low-key cafés and restaurants that feature within the routes and are intended to offer a wider choice for evening dining. Also included here are some nightlife listings and our recommendations for books and films about the destination.

ABOUT THE AUTHORS

Patrick Kinsella is a freelance journalist and editor who has the outrageously good fortune to be a dual citizen of Australia and the UK, enabling him to enjoy the delights of both and experience their vastly contrasting wonders with new eyes each time he swaps hemispheres. Researching this book before he even knew he'd be writing it, he spent most of the last decade living in Melbourne, enjoying the world's best coffee culture and unwrapping Australia's most interesting city one fascinating layer at a time. This book builds on original content by Virginia Maxwell, a native Melburnian with a love for the city's vibrant café culture, exciting contemporary architecture and wonderful bookshops.

CONTACT THE EDITORS

We hope you find this Explore Guide useful, interesting and a pleasure to read. If you have any questions or feedback on the text, pictures or maps, please do let us know. If you have noticed any errors or outdated facts, or have suggestions for places to include on the routes, we would be delighted to hear from you. Please drop us an email at hello@insightguides.com. Thanks!

CREDITS

Explore Melbourne

Contributors: Patrick Kinsella and Virginia Maxwell

Commissioning Editor: Sarah Clark

Pictures: Tom Smyth

Map Production: original cartography Stephen Ramsay, updated by Apa Cartography Department

Production: Rebeka Davies and Aga Bylica

Photo credits: Alamy 136; Corbis 48/49; David Simmonds/Fed Square 42; Downtowner 107; Fotolia 86/87; Getty Images 2/3T, 5T, 6/7T, 24/25, 26/27T, 26MC, 34, 40, 56, 68, 73, 91, 93L, 98/99T; Gil Meydan 33; Glyn Genin/Apa Publications 17; Greg Gladman/Apa Publications 51; Hellenic Republic 115, 116; Hilton Hotels & Resorts 100, 101L; iStock 1, 4ML, 9, 35, 65, 80, 81, 86, 96/97, 129, 134/135; James Geer 30, 30/31; Jasper Hotel 102; Jeremy Simons 98ML; Jerry Dennis/Apa Publications 2MC, 2MR, 2MR, 2ML, 4MC, 4BC, 5M, 5MR, 6ML, 6MC, 6MR, 6MR, 8, 10, 10/11, 11L, 12, 14/15, 15L, 16, 18, 23, 26ML, 26MC, 26MR, 26ML, 26MR, 28, 28/29, 29L, 31L, 38, 39, 42/43, 43L, 44, 45, 46, 50, 52, 53, 57, 58, 59, 60, 62, 63L, 66, 69, 70, 70/71, 71L, 72, 74/75, 76, 76/77, 77L, 78/79, 82, 82/83, 83L, 84, 85, 88, 89, 90, 95, 94, 98ML, 98MR, 98MC, 104, 108, 110, 124/125, 126, 128, 130, 131, 132, 133; John Gollings/Fed Square 5MR, 41; Langham Hotels 102/103, 103L; Leonardo 106; MoVida 98MC, 111; National Gallery of Victoria 67; National Sports Museum 2ML, 62/63; Nobu 117, 118; Prince Bandroom 122/123; Ristorarte Via Margutta 6ML; Sarti 112, 114; Screen Australia/The Kobal Collection 137; Stamford Plaza 105; Stokehouse 6MC, 119; Taxi Dining Room 113; The Adelphi 100/101; The Prince 109; Virginia Star/Apa Publications 4TL, 13, 20, 21L, 20/21, 22, 32, 36/37, 47, 54, 55, 61, 64, 78, 79L, 87L, 92, 92/93, 98MR, 120, 121, 127; Visions of Victoria 2MC, 14, 19

Cover credits: Corbis (main); Dreamstime (bottom)

DISTRIBUTION

Worldwide

APA Publications GmbH & Co. Verlag KG (Singapore branch)

7030 Ang Mo Kio Ave 5, 08-65

Northstar @ AMK, Singapore 569880

Email: apasin@singnet.com.sg

UK and Ireland

Dorling Kindersley Ltd (a Penguin Company)

80 Strand, London, WC2R 0RL, UK

Email: sales@uk.dk.com

US

Ingram Publisher Services

One Ingram Blvd, PO Box 3006, La Vergne, TN 37086-1986

Email: ips@ingramcontent.com

Australia and New Zealand

Woodslane

10 Apollo St, Warriewood NSW 2102, Australia

Email: info@woodslane.com.au

INDEX

MAP LEGEND

- Start of tour
→ Tour & route direction
❶ Recommended sight
❷ Recommended restaurant/café

★ Place of interest
❶ Tourist information
𝟏 Statue/monument
✉ Main post office
🚌 Main bus station
↯ Viewpoint

Park
Important building
Hotel
Transport hub
Market/store
Pedestrian area
Urban area